PRAISE FOR *WORKQUAKE*

"The shocks to the workplace from COVID-19 are just the latest example of an increasingly dynamic and ever-changing labor marketplace. Similar to what we see at Glassdoor, *Workquake* shows that the companies best set up to succeed in this environment are those that play the long game by investing and building positive relationships with their employees."

CHRISTIAN SUTHERLAND-WONG, CEO, GLASSDOOR

"With the pace of change continuing to accelerate all around us, it's time to rip up the old playbooks and reconsider what attributes we'll need in order to thrive professionally. In *Workquake*, Steve blends his considerable personal experiences with relevant research and insightful stories to create highly compelling guidelines for navigating the future of work. Steve's style is engaging, and his advice hits the spot."

LEELA SRINIVASAN, BOARD MEMBER, UPWORK

"The old contract of work is dead. *Workquake* will challenge you to pursue learning agility over job security and to paradoxically build a company culture that prepares people to leave."

MICHELLE VITUS, FOUNDER AND CEO, SLATE ADVISERS

"Nothing is more essential in our lives than the terms and conditions of work, and nothing has been so profoundly disrupted over the last thirty years. Steve Cadigan begins with basic human motives—to prosper, grow, and explore—and offers sage advice to employees and employers. An empowering book for those seeking to understand how to navigate careers and life in a rapidly changing world."

CHARLES MOSES, DEAN, SCHOOL OF MANAGEMENT, UNIVERSITY OF SAN FRANCISCO

"In *Workquake* Steve Cadigan lays bare the obsolete social compact that has bound employees to employers since the Industrial Revolution. Using poignant examples from his own career and extensive quotes from enlightened CEOs, entrepreneurs, and other contemporary leaders, Cadigan offers the outline for a fundamental shift from a system based on loyalty and tenure to a more open system based on trust and a better understanding of the employment 'long-game.' The book is written in two parts—one for employees, and one for employers—but Cadigan encourages everyone to read both. I would add one more category to his list: educators. The book is full of challenges to the way we teach and prepare students for the modern world of work. While he tackles an incredibly complex subject, Cadigan's writing is clear, direct, and full of stories that make the message memorable. But perhaps most importantly, Cadigan is optimistic about the future of work when, as he puts it, 'Most of the discussion about the future of work today tends to be dismal.' The world of work is getting better, and in *Workquake*, Steve Cadigan clearly shows us how to accelerate that trend."

JOHN HAGGERTY, SR. LECTURER, CORNELL UNIVERSITY ILR;
FORMER VP HUMAN RESOURCES, GENERAL ELECTRIC

"An inspirational read about the future of work—at times of great uncertainty and change. Steve makes a compelling argument about how to understand and embrace change to get ready for the future that awaits us. Contrary to what you might think, it is less about technological advancement and more about leveraging values that make us humans."

TOLGA KURTOGLU, CEO, XEROX PARC

"In this very refreshing and easy-to-read book, Steve provides compelling examples of how today's most successful workers and employers embrace constant learning, change, and career flexibility. Written by a man who is regarded as a thought leader on the subject, this is a must-read if you want to thrive in this fast-changing new world order!"

KIRK HERRINGTON, CEO AND BOARD MEMBER, MPLOY

"For both employers and employees, managing the velocity of change in work and careers is one of the central challenges of business today. Steve Cadigan provides a vital path forward on this complex topic that is practical, optimistic, and deeply humane. It's an indispensable read for those serious about the future of work."

PETER CAMPBELL, MANAGING PARTNER,
EDUCATION GROWTH PARTNERS

"Technology and changing social values have radically changed our labor function. In California, voters passed a law validating 'gig' labor as a new form of labor. It's time to rethink old strategies for managing the employer–employee relationship, and Steve Cadigan does that beautifully in this book! Workquake is a must-read for all business and HR leaders."

JANINE YANCEY, FOUNDER AND CEO, EMTRAIN

"In this extraordinary time of upheaval, we are being forced to re-evaluate many things. Questions around work-life balance, mental health, family, and more secure income are high on that list, but we must reconcile these questions with realizations, like the absolute necessity to develop hyper flexibility in the face of disruption, to embrace concepts like the gig economy, and to face the intriguing notion that perhaps you are not what you do. Steve Cadigan guides us through this changing world with a sense of creativity and optimism that's inspiring and invigorating, and I recommend *Workquake* as required reading for all of us."

PATRICK CRANE, BOARD MEMBER, TECHNOLOGY EXECUTIVE

"As we have been building Certn, we have found Steve's insights to be a total paradigm shift for the company. His teachings are enormously valuable in helping us nail the right talent strategies to compete for and hire great talent. *Workquake* reveals many of his game-changing strategies and is a must-read for entrepreneurs and professionals."

ANDREW MCLEOD, FOUNDER AND C3O, CERTN

"Steve was the head of 'player personnel' at PMC-Sierra. He drove a 'big H' HR program that prioritized driving the right kind of culture and talent for our company versus just hiring and replacing people by numbers. *Workquake* is very timely and should be a must-read for every organization trying to navigate these unprecedented times."

BOB BAILEY, DIRECTOR, MICRON;

FORMER CHAIRMAN AND CEO, PMC-SIERRA

"Unequivocally, Steve is one of the world's pre-eminent experts on the future of work. He provides a unique combination of fresh, challenging concepts and practical, tangible solutions born out of his experience as a top-level HR leader. A master storyteller. *Workquake* is a must-read."

ADRIAN SIMPSON, CO-FOUNDER AND CHIEF CONNECTOR,

WAVELENGTH

"In the doom and gloom around the future of work, *Workquake* shines a bright, optimistic light on the opportunity for young people to navigate an ever-changing workplace. The book breaks down the employee-employer relationship and encourages you to think about the value of humans in leveraging technology. A must-read, especially for college students who are looking for answers to questions of the future."

ASHWATH NARAYANAN, FOUNDER AND CEO, SOCIAL CURRANT

"Steve starts with what is—where people are, and what's true about work, the workplace, and employers today, not what was or what should be. Then, through his compelling use of real-world stories and penetrating insight, he keeps you engaged while laying out what needs to be true to maximize work outcomes for employee and employer alike. This is a bright light provided by one whose expertise is built on firsthand experience and the determination to grow people and companies."

MATT BARNARD, CO-FOUNDER AND CEO, PLENTY

WORKQUAKE

www.amplifypublishing.com

Workquake: Embracing the Aftershocks of COVID-19 to Create a Better Model of Working

For more information, please contact:
Amplify Publishing, an imprint of Mascot Books
620 Herndon Parkway #320
Herndon, VA 20170
info@amplifypublishing.com

Library of Congress Control Number: 2021900739

CPSIA Code: PRFRE0321A
ISBN-13: 978-1-64543-426-9

Printed in Canada

The future of work is not about robots, AI, and automation. The future of work is about being more human.

—Steve Cadigan

Jenny, Carson, Connor, Spencer, Trevor, Allie, and Carley—you are my life force, my inspiration, and my joy. You are the reason life has meaning, and I strive every day to make you proud of me.

Dad, Mom, Linda, Katie, Mark, Anne, and John—you are the best family I could have hoped to be raised within, and I count my blessings every day for your love and the lives we have all built as a family. We are all the products of those around us, and every one of you has made me a better person.

FOREWORD BY ALAN WEBBER,
CO-FOUNDER, *FAST COMPANY*

WORKQUAKE

EMBRACING THE AFTERSHOCKS OF COVID-19 TO CREATE A BETTER MODEL OF WORKING

STEVE CADIGAN

CONTENTS

FOREWORD

WORKQUAKE: WHY YOU NEED TO READ THIS BOOK

Alan Webber, co-founder, Fast Company magazine;
former managing editor, Harvard Business Review; Mayor of Santa Fe,
New Mexico

Most introductions to books begin by talking about the themes and messages that make the book worth reading.

I want to begin by talking about the man who wrote the book and why he makes the book worth reading.

Why start with the writer and not the writing?

Because of one of the underlying themes in this book: the democratization of work and the proliferation of choice. On the face of it, both of these developments represent genuinely positive contributions to our lives. Employment, careers, personal growth, and personal development are all opening up new paths and allowing each of us to discover our own gifts, passions, and talents. More choice allows more people to try new things rather than feeling locked in and locked down by the dictates of the past or the demands of the status quo.

But there's always a "but," and there are always two sides to the same coin. In this case, if one side is more freedom of choice and greater access to information, the other side is confusion and randomness in the presence of so much choice. Faced with the blurring of old boundaries and the elimination of old rules, confronted with more voices offering more choices, how do we know whom to listen to and which advice to follow?

For me it comes down to trust. I simply can't follow advice from someone I don't trust. Trust is a must. And I want you to know: you can trust Steve Cadigan. I've known Steve for more than a decade, and I consider myself enormously fortunate to call him a friend. He is not only a "friend of the road"—we all have these, folks we meet along life's journey, share some experiences with, and then lose touch with as paths diverge. Steve is a "friend of the heart"—a friend whose life story, values, and personal qualities make him a steadfast companion for the duration of this journey. Over the last decade, I've seen Steve's career reflect everything he writes about in this book. I've watched with great respect and appreciation as Steve has created for himself the very changes he writes about in regard to all of us in our work and our careers. His work life makes him a living example of the message he is offering us. If you want to know why you should listen to him, the answer is simple: he lives what he says.

And there's another reason that ties closely to another deep theme in this book: we no longer separate our lives into work and life. Who we are, what we do, and how we do it are all intertwined. Character and competence, courage, and capability are all manifestations of the essential measures of any individual.

Over the last decade, I've seen Steve—not as a professional but as a person—take on the challenges that come to all of us in life. He and I have talked about family, children, marriage, health, self-awareness—all the difficulties that each of us must deal with. We've talked about the fact that in this life "no one walks away unscathed." It's not a question of whether or even when it's your turn to deal with the pain that living brings (to quote Bruce Springsteen). It's a question of how you deal with it when it's your turn.

I trust and believe what Steve says about work and careers, employers and employees, not just because of what Steve knows, but even more because of who Steve is. He is the real deal, and what he says stands up for that reason.

Now, what is it that he's telling us in this book? And why is the message as worthy as the messenger?

Steve's book begins with the inescapable truth of our time: everything is changing. Make your own list; here's a start: work is changing. Careers are changing. The shape, structure, trajectory, and value of jobs are all changing. Companies are changing —even to the point of losing track of what constitutes a company. For a long time, a lot of things in business were more or less done and settled. We all knew how competition was structured and how to map the forces at work. We all knew how value was created and how to capture it. Roles and responsibilities were defined, functions delineated, practices and policies described and settled.

Change has been the order of the day—or the disorder of the day—for at least the last thirty years, since around the time that Bill Taylor and I started *Fast Company* magazine with the thought that we were creating the magazine that would chronicle the changes that were beginning to disrupt the world of business. In our first letter from the editors, we wrote, "The world is changing, and business is changing the world."

Today, that seems like a timid understatement. Everything—everything—is up for reimagination, reconsideration, reinvention. Disruption is everywhere.

There's a famous quote from Ernest Hemingway's *The Sun Also Rises* that captures the way change has captured us. "How did you go bankrupt?" one character asks another. "Two ways," another answers. "Gradually, then suddenly."

That's the world we live in now. We saw change coming—gradually—until we arrived at a completely new world of work, suddenly.

And now, as I write this, we are in a world of change that is compounded by a world changed by change. COVID-19, a global pandemic, has spawned a global financial crisis, which has demanded that we confront a past of racial injustices, social inequities, and institutionalized discriminations. In this time of change, we are each one of us asked to explore what's right and true for ourselves while examining what is right and true for all of us.

But what Steve sees clearly and unflinchingly is not only how important this new reckoning is. He also sees what an unparalleled opportunity it is.

How often does a time of disruption like this come along? As Steve accurately says, we have the opportunity and the responsibility to step into this time with courage and with confidence. We have a once-in-a-lifetime chance to arrive at new ways of working and new ways of behaving. We can take these compounding disruptions and arrive at new codes for ourselves and for our children that emphasize not only personal opportunity but also collective fairness.

We all need to read this book for what it tells us about our time and ourselves. We also need to read this book for the conversations it must start, for the principles it provides, and for the guideposts it offers as we go forward.

Change is the underlying message of this book, and it is the underlying reality of our time. Change is going to last; change will keep coming, and it is up to us to keep moving toward it, into it, and with it.

In a time of change, what we need more than anything else is a trusted guide, an accomplished and experienced practitioner of the art of change.

We are so fortunate to have that guide, that voice, that steady hand in Steve Cadigan.

Please read this book. Please tell others that they should read it too. And then we all need to embrace it, learn from it, and keep moving with it as we confront the next wave of change. And then the next.

ALAN WEBBER
August 2020

INTRODUCTION

MY AWAKENING

It was late in the summer of 2009 at about eight in the morning, and I was walking onto the beautiful campus at Electronic Arts (EA) in Redwood City, California, heading toward my office. I was a vice president of human resources and had joined EA about fifteen months earlier. Suddenly, my phone rang, and I could see it was my boss, Gabrielle (Gaby) Toledano. I took the call, and before I could finish even saying, "Hi, Gaby," she exclaimed, "I know you are interviewing at LinkedIn!" My heart sank, my blood pressure immediately rose, and my internal voice said, *Oh no! How did she find out? If I don't get the job at LinkedIn, I am so dead!* I will never forget that moment, because it ignited a journey that led me to write this book. Let me explain.

In early 2008 I had been approached by EA about an opportunity to join their team as VP of HR for a large division of the company and to assume a leadership role for their ambitious plans to acquire and integrate some large game studios around the world. Earlier in my career, I had led the acquisition integration team for Cisco, and I loved the challenge of acquisition integration work. The video game industry had a real appeal to me, and EA had recently appointed a new CEO, John Riccitiello. Riccitiello's big plans to grow the company through big deals appealed to me. I was offered and accepted the job. However, not long after I started, the grim reality of the second mortgage crisis hit, a global recession began, and EA had to scrap their ambitious acquisition plans. This meant the job I was hired for suddenly became way less attractive.

These factors led me to consider an opportunity to be the first chief HR officer at LinkedIn. A few days before the call from Gaby, I was interviewed by every member of the LinkedIn executive team, and it was love at first sight. I wanted that job badly. After the interviews I wanted to show the LinkedIn executives I was savvy about their technology and how the site worked, so I immediately sent everyone a personalized thank-you and a request to join their networks. The day after I posted my invitations, every single member of the LinkedIn executive team accepted my invitations to join their networks, and I was pumped! *This is a good omen*, I thought. *This is a good sign that I might get the job.*

What I did not realize, though, was how the LinkedIn technology actually worked. You see, back then, once you added someone to your network, LinkedIn sent a message to everyone in your network that you had added someone new, and it even listed who the person was, their title, and their place of employment. I did not realize that the day after my connection requests were accepted, my entire network would receive a message essentially saying, "Steve Cadigan is now connected to the chairman, CEO, CFO, general counsel, VP of product, VP of engineering, VP of sales, VP of operations, and VP of marketing at

LinkedIn." It would not take a genius to see that I was probably interviewing there. My efforts to impress my potential new employer resulted in my boss finding out I was interviewing. Oops!

So there I was, standing in the lobby. My boss was on the phone, obviously upset. *How did I let this happen?* I asked myself. *How could I not realize she would find out?* I also felt awful because Gaby had been a great boss and had treated me exceptionally well. It was not her fault or my fault that the economic recession had made my job less appealing. I hated feeling like I had let her down. And while the feelings of dread filled my head, what was bothering me more started to become apparent. Gaby and I were both upset because we were actors in a system that we both knew was not realistic. I kept thinking, *Why am I feeling so bad when I should be excited about a great opportunity at LinkedIn?* I was not happy at work because my job had diminished, so I had explored a new opportunity at LinkedIn. That was entirely fair and reasonable.

I was supposed to feel bad because, according to the "system" that Gaby and I were playing in, I was breaking an unspoken rule. According to the way the employer-employee relationship should have worked, we were expected to stay with employers more than the fifteen months I had been at EA, so the prospect of me breaking that expectation was going to have ramifications for my boss and me. I never signed a contract with EA to stay a long time, and they never committed to employing me for a long time. But we both operated with that expectation. This gnawed at me. Something just didn't feel right. It did not feel honest. It was right at that moment I realized the old employer-employee contract was broken. I realized I was stuck feeling awful because of an old model.

I immediately headed to Gaby's office, and I told her everything about my situation. My heart felt like it was in my throat. I felt awful. I had no idea if LinkedIn would hire me or not, and I was unsure if my situation at EA was recoverable if I did not get the job. I felt vulnerable and afraid. Fortunately for me, Gaby was a true professional. She understood my situation, and we had spoken previously about how unhappy I was at EA. I just hadn't told her I was actively interviewing for another job.

After we both laid our cards on the table, I started to feel bad for Gaby because I knew she was going to take heat if I did leave EA "so early." She was going to take heat because the system we were working in expected leaders to keep their employees, and as the HR exec in charge, Gaby had to set the bar for the rest of the leaders at EA, who were also expected to keep their people. Gaby said personally she very much supported me, and I believed her, so we were able to have an "off-the-record" conversation that further served to cement in my mind that we were in a game where the rules did not fit the reality of the situation.

As it turned out, I received an offer to join LinkedIn, and I accepted. However, I will never forget how that conversation with Gaby made me question the system of employment I was working within. That experience served to open my eyes to an employer-employee relationship that seemed fundamentally flawed. Why couldn't we have had a more open conversation instead of a private understanding? Why did the system serve to give Gaby heat when it should have praised her for grooming me and coaching me to a bigger and better opportunity?* Why

---

* If leaders are measured by how well their staff do after they leave that leader, Gaby Toledano would be near the top of most lists. Gaby's former employees have gone on to be heads of HR for the following companies: LinkedIn, Zynga, LivingSocial, CBS Interactive, GoPro, Rocket Fuel, Shutterfly, ModCloth, Minted, Anaplan, Hootsuite, and Coca-Cola Europe. And the list of companies where other talent has moved

was I made to feel disloyal and almost like a traitor for leaving? I had never promised to stay at EA for a long time, and they had made no promises to me that I would have a long career there, but there was an outdated expectation that both of us would believe a commitment existed, even when we both knew it wasn't realistic. Leaving a senior position before two years was not my plan, but staying in a job that felt half as interesting as it was before the recession was not part of my plan either.

This moment served as the awakening that led me to undertake writing this book. I felt a seismic shift was taking place in the employer-employee relationship. Why can't we have relationships with companies and employees that are based on the probability that we are going to separate, not the illusion that we won't? Why can't we have a model that would have allowed EA to celebrate my move to LinkedIn openly? We both knew the model did not work—but what could we do about it? How many people in the world find themselves in situations where the employment model does not suit the reality of an economy that is changing faster than ever? In this economy, where promises of anything long term are unrealistic, how can either party commit to anything long-term? This experience ignited my mission to build a better model for today—a better, more honest, employer-employee relationship.

---

from EA to bigger roles includes impressive names like Apple, Netflix, and McKesson, to name a few. Unfortunately, old models of the employer-employee relationship don't allow these great progressions to be celebrated. EA has been a wonderful growth experience for many HR leaders.

A LANDSCAPE OF FEAR

Fear by itself is not a "bad" emotion any more than happiness is a "good" one. What matters is the degree to which we feel these emotions and how they impact the choices we make in any given situation.

For example, should a grizzly bear come charging straight at you, the natural evolutionary instinct for self-preservation would prompt you to climb the nearest tree or run down a hill (grizzlies can't easily climb or run downhill). That's a good thing. But experience too much fear, and you might not do anything at all—or maybe too much, like trying to fight the bear with your bare hands. Either way, that's a bad thing.

At the risk of metaphorical excess, the grizzly bear is our technology-driven economy. And many employees and employers are the scared hikers in the woods.

We live in an era of unprecedented technological change. The pace of innovation has rapidly accelerated, making business models and whole industries quickly obsolete. While every company strives for competitive advantage today through some form of digital innovation, lost in this dramatic advancement has been the simple reality that all this change has created a scary frontier for both professionals *and* employers.

This rapid technological advancement makes it impossible for individuals and organizations to predict what skills they need for the future, a situation we as a society have never previously faced.

This phenomenon has become known as the "skills gap," in which the pace of technological change exceeds society's ability to learn the skills needed to apply the new technology. While technology has always disrupted the economy and displaced workers, the gap between what employers need and what employees can provide is significant, is accelerating, and shows no sign of shrinking.*

By 2025 the economy will have created 133 million jobs that do not exist today, according to the World Economic Forum.†

For professionals and employees today, education and experience no longer guarantee long-term employment. For employers, long-term planning is all but irrelevant. An unknown future fills both employee and employer with fear and anxiety.

As a result, the relationship between employees and employers is fundamentally changing as both parties strive to find their footing within an uncertain future.

> *The relationship between employees and employers is fundamentally changing as both parties strive to find their footing within an uncertain future.*

Employees are leaving their jobs at quicker rates. In 2018 the *median* job tenure for employees between the age of twenty-five and thirty-five years of age in the United States was just 2.8 years, according to the Federal Bureau of Labor Statistics.‡ Do that math. This means that half the working population between the ages of twenty-five and thirty-five are staying with their employers less than 2.8 years!

Organizations around the world no longer make promises of long-term employment. In 2019 I held workshops in San Francisco, Portugal, Madrid, Barcelona, and Mexico City, where

---

* https://hbr.org/2014/08/employers-arent-just-whining-the-skills-gap-is-real.
† https://www.weforum.org/focus/skills-for-your-future.
‡ https://www.bls.gov/news.release/tenure.nr0.htm.

I asked CEOs if they offered the prospect of a "long career" to potential employees. Not a single hand went up. Not one. And when I inquired as to why nobody was offering any guarantees of employment anymore, the answer was the same in every country: "The future is too unpredictable," hence it's impossible to know what skills you will need down the road to compete.

Such long-term commitments could handicap a company if the economy and/or technological changes force CEOs to shift direction suddenly. Yet many CEOs also complain that employees no longer possess loyalty. They blame the so-called millennial generation* for having a short attention span and wanting a quick fix promotion as the main drivers of employees leaving employers faster today. But how can CEOs expect loyalty when they can't guarantee job security to their employees? The game is changing, and the contract between employer and employee is not what it used to be.

FEAR OF IRRELEVANCE

Of course, people have many good reasons to switch jobs, such as better pay or a promotion. But I suspect a primary reason driving employees to change jobs today stems from the fear that they are not learning enough to maintain their employability and remain relevant. If they think that a move to a different firm makes them more valuable for tomorrow, they will make a move. Loyalty today seems to be swinging away from a company and toward anything that will ensure a person can remain relevant and employable in an uncertain future.

---

*   https://www.tlnt.com/the-millennial-turnover-myth-why-young-talent-really-decides-to-leave/.

Traditional models of careers have been based on the notion that job security comes from being stationary within one firm for an extended period—building your credibility with long-term commitments and loyalty over time. You were seen as more relevant and valuable if you could demonstrate long-term employment. Today, the notion of job security has shifted from being stationary to being in movement.

> *Today, the notion of job security has shifted from being stationary to being in movement.*

The more you change jobs, the more you build your network, the more you are exposed to new business models, the more you are likely to learn new things, and the more you learn, the more valuable you become. This is the primary reason why I believe more and more people are changing jobs faster today than at any point in history. *Employees are increasingly adopting the notion that the more I move, the more I learn, and the more valuable I become in a world of work that is rapidly changing and where there are no promises of long-term employment.* This is *not* a millennial-generation phenomenon; this is a new reality primarily created by the rapid advancement of technology and the fast pace with which industries and companies can be disrupted.

The fear that AI, robots, and automation will replace human employees serves to heighten this anxiety. As a result, people are flocking to a host of new nanodegree programs and e-learning schools such as Udacity and Singularity. Research and markets predict that the e-learning market will reach $325 billion by 2025.[*]

---

[*] https://elearningindustry.com/top-elearning-statistics-2019.

Let's all take a deep breath. If the unknown fuels fear and anxiety, then we should focus on what we do know. Understanding the source of our dread will demystify it and help us craft strategies on how to move forward.

Throughout human history, technological innovation has consistently disrupted economies. From the printing press and power loom to the automobile and personal computer, technology has destroyed industries but also created new ones.

The United States has always boasted a unique relationship with labor. The concept of the American dream meant that people, no matter their socioeconomic background, could obtain prosperity through merit and a strong work ethic.

After the Industrial Revolution, many companies adopted a paternalistic relationship with their workers, meaning employers cared for their employees like extended family but demanded absolute loyalty and obedience in return. Hence the birth of company towns like Hershey in Pennsylvania and Pullman in Illinois.

The automobile industry—including General Motors, Ford, and Chrysler—offered their employees a path toward the middle class with good pay, benefits, and job security. Throughout the Midwest, multiple generations of families worked the assembly lines in Detroit. Work was the path to a dream destination. As long as you were loyal, hardworking, and put in your time, your future would be set. The company had your back.

Throughout these decades, work evolved from just a means to an end to the end itself. Perhaps more than any other country in the world, Americans, especially college-educated professionals, associate their self-worth with their jobs. Work gives Americans a sense of purpose and identity.

"The economists of the early twentieth century did not

foresee that work might evolve from a means of material production to a means of identity production," Derick Thompson recently wrote for *The Atlantic* magazine. "They failed to anticipate that, for the poor and middle class, work would remain a necessity; but for the college-educated elite, it would morph into a kind of religion, promising identity, transcendence, and community. Call it workism."*

In many ways, the aspirational American dream ethos, employees' historical dependence on employers, and worship of work have conspired to make us ill-suited, at least psychologically, for the challenges of the twenty-first-century digital economy.

Computing has become both faster and cheaper, which makes industries easier to disrupt. What it costs to build a company today and the time it takes to build an organization are both far less than at any other time in history. For big employers, this is a scary reality. Globalization and free trade mean workers from both rich and developing countries must compete with each other.

And since 2000, we have experienced two recessions, including the 2007 financial crisis, which, before COVID-19, led to the worst economic downturn since the Great Depression. The lack of stability is the new norm, and we're neither emotionally nor intellectually equipped to manage this rapid change.

LESS FEAR, MORE SOLUTIONS

I have grown weary of reading all the doom and gloom stories about the future of work. Yes, robots, AI, and automation are

---

*   https://www.theatlantic.com/ideas/archive/2019/02/religion-workism-making-americans-miserable/583441/.

changing the economy and the nature of work, but that's not the most important conversation for us to have right now. We have done a very poor job marketing new technology and digital transformations. The way the digital revolution is being sold to us in the media is that millions of jobs will be lost and people will be out of work. That is unproductive. The more important conversation is: What does all this change mean to us, to our jobs, to our careers, and to our employers? What can we do about this workquake?

Employability is the new job security.

I wanted to write this book to start finding solutions. With the right mindset and strategies, both employer and employee can move beyond fear and anxiety.

Employees need to recognize that employability is the new job security. The focus should move away from trying to keep your job and move toward ensuring you are developing and growing so that you are employable and immune to disruptions and unexpected changes that may force your company to let you go. Professionals must be able to adapt on the fly consistently. To stay relevant, they must proactively acquire new knowledge, skills, and professional networks on an ongoing basis.

The same principle applies to employers. Companies today must be willing to disrupt themselves before a competitor or new technology does. In this context, disruption means much more than changing an organization's products, operations, or communications. Employers must also adopt new models of recruiting, training, and compensation to attract an increasingly nomadic workforce.

For example, most employers have historically focused on employee retention. When I worked for Cisco and EA, my bonus partly depended on how well we prevented our best employees from leaving. Employers today still tie benefits, whether retirement payouts or paid time off, to how long workers stay at the company. But this practice is no longer realistic in the digital economy.

> *Organizations need to shift their thinking away from "How do we keep our staff from leaving?" and move it toward "How do we make our people better for an uncertain future?"*

Instead, we must redefine the relationship between employer and employee. We can no longer operate under the traditional model of a nine-to-five, Monday-to-Friday, forty-hours-a-week job in which the employer merely supplies pay and benefits in exchange for labor.

Instead, we need a new compact that emphasizes flexibility, training, and job experiences and allows each side to navigate an uncertain future confidently. We need a new agreement that resonates with both employers and employees. Organizations need to shift their thinking away from "How do we keep our staff from leaving?" and move it toward "How do we make our people better for an uncertain future?"

We all fear that machines will replace us. Yet creativity, innovation, communication, and adaptation remain critical to forging a strong economy. That means humans and being fundamentally human have never been more essential to work, especially in a world that often overestimates what technology can accomplish.

Together we can create a future of work rooted not in fear but rather in our shared humanity. We can build a new model that feels far more satisfying than the one we share today. I hope you will join me in this effort.

1

TIME TO BE MORE HUMAN

EMBRACING AMBIGUITY

There is a popular technique in acting called improv. Through a series of exercises and role-playing games, actors are placed into random situations where they must make up dialogue on the spot.

For example, in one game called "freeze," two actors are portraying, say, a doctor talking to his patient. They start improvising their dialogue until another actor not in the scene yells, "Freeze!" That person walks into the scene and replaces one of the original actors. Once the action resumes, the new actor, assuming the physical stance of the person he has just replaced, starts a new scene with entirely different characters and circumstances.

As you can imagine, there can be an endless number of possibilities with improv. There's only one rule: you can't say no. You may have been initially playing a doctor talking to his patient, but now you're a father scolding his son. Whether you like that scene or not, you must go with it.

At first glance, you might think the point of improv is to stimulate creativity. That's not wrong. But improv's real value is to get actors comfortable with ambiguity. You get comfortable with one scene and then—*boom!* Someone changes it into something else. You must accept without reservation whatever your fellow actors give you at any particular moment.

Ambiguity and acting would seem like strange bedfellows. After all, the actor repeats the same lines of a play every night, interacts with the same cast, wears the same costumes, sings the same songs, and dances the same choreography.

But any actor would tell you that theater is rarely static. Anything can happen during a show. The audience may respond differently to a particular performance, laughing one night and being stone-cold silent the next.

The actor may discover new insight into his character, which forces other actors to respond appropriately. Things may go wrong: an actor forgets a piece of dialogue, the orchestra misses a music cue, or the stage manager forgets to put a crucial prop on the table.

It's no wonder that many employers hire actors to conduct improv workshops for executives and employees alike. In today's digital economy, things change on the fly, and employers and employees must adapt accordingly.

Like actors, we can't say no to a new situation. We have to accept the change. And we certainly can't yell, "Freeze!" in real life, no matter how much we want to.

The show must go on.

WE DON'T LIKE AMBIGUITY

As human beings, we simply don't like ambiguity. We demand definite answers to subjective, even unanswerable questions. Is this person good or bad? Is the character dead or alive at the end of the movie? Does my boss like or hate me?

Even the concept of time is steeped in ambiguity. Before Albert Einstein's groundbreaking special theory of relativity, we assumed time was absolute, that it moved in a predictable, constant fashion. But Einstein taught us that time moves at different rates depending on the speed of motion and the vantage point of the particular observer.

Our brain processes an extraordinary amount of information from our senses: what we see, hear, smell, touch, and taste. But that information is often incomplete. As a result, the brain "fills in the blank" with its best guess. It's one reason why two witnesses might tell completely different stories even though they observed the same event.

Ambiguity makes us uncomfortable, anxious, and even angry. Humans find repetition and consistency much easier to absorb than fluctuation or randomness. Further, as humans, we find comfort in a consistent, reliable, and safe reality, especially as we age, and that is mostly a survival instinct we have embedded within us.

In 1949 psychologists Jerome Bruner and Leo Postman at Harvard University published a now-famous study that explored how people responded to unexpected information.

The researchers asked participants to quickly identify playing cards they flashed to them. Among some regular cards were trick cards designed to confuse people: three of hearts (black), four of hearts (black), two of spades (red), six of spades (red), ace of diamonds (black), and six of clubs (red).

Bruner and Postman discovered that participants responded to the trick cards with a mixture of frustration and denial, insisting that a red six of spades shown to them was really a black six of spades or red six of hearts.

Another typical response was confusion followed by a loss of confidence: "I can't make the suit out, whatever it is. It didn't even look like a card at that time. I don't know what color it is now or whether it's a spade or heart. I'm not even sure now what a spade looks like! My God!"

In other words, we are so used to seeing black clubs/spades and red hearts/diamonds in a deck of cards that anything that breaks those expectations throws us for a loop.

The same can be said about our careers.

Society has long taught us that we follow a sequence of events: go to college, pick a major, and become a lawyer, doctor, firefighter, accountant, or electrician. We have been programmed to choose a single path that we believe will provide us with safety, security, and reliability. And if it doesn't, the fault, sadly, lies with the person.

> *The average person will change careers five to seven times during their working life.*

But that assumption is just not realistic today. According to one study,* the average person will change careers five to seven times during their working life. Not necessarily because he or she wants to but rather because he or she has to.

The Great Recession of 2007 to 2009—the worst economic downturn in America since the Great Depression—was so

---

*   https://careers-advice-online.com/career-change-statistics.html.

severe that some economists speculate it may have created a permanent class of well-educated but perpetually underemployed Americans who have delayed or abandoned their career plans altogether.

The traditional career path has been disrupted by technology, specifically the birth of low-cost cloud computing, which has allowed companies to innovate and disrupt industries faster—and more cheaply—than ever before. Technology that people consider breakthrough one week may become obsolete in a matter of months. The progress is both magnificent and terrifying.

The once unmistakable line from education to quality, stable employment now seems mighty fuzzy.

"These days, the culprit preventing many professionals from identifying a clear career path at their company is simply that one no longer exists," Dorie Clark, a marketing strategist and adjunct professor at Duke University, wrote in *Harvard Business Review*.

> *These days, the culprit preventing many professionals from identifying a clear career path at their company is simply that one no longer exists.*
>
> —Dorrie Clark

"Given that successful companies must often pivot to adapt to changes in the marketplace and the half-life of many skills is now estimated to be five years or less, companies often have no idea what staffing needs they'll have in a few years' time or who would be qualified to fill them."

In the past you could reasonably expect the knowledge and skills you acquired during college would last your entire career.

You could also reasonably expect your work experience would increase your professional value. No longer. Eighty-five percent of jobs that will exist in 2030 do not exist today, according to The Future of Work Institute.* Besides, 65 percent of students today will work jobs that have yet to be created.

No wonder we're so depressed.

MENTAL HEALTH WORRIES

In 2017 about 17.3 million US adults, or 7.1 percent of all adults, suffered from major depression, according to data from the National Institute of Mental Health.† Major depression is the leading disability for people between ages 15 and 44.3.‡

Anxiety is even worse. The disorder impacts 40 million US adults each year, or 18.1 percent of the population.

Data also suggests that teenagers are already feeling the worries of an uncertain job market and economic future.

A recent survey§ by the Pew Research Center found that 70 percent of people ages thirteen to seventeen named depression and anxiety as the top concern among teenagers today. One possible reason for these feelings is that society dictates we must follow a specific path to achieve success and stability. Indeed, 61 percent of teens said they felt a lot of pressure to get good grades.

---

* https://www.delltechnologies.com/content/dam/delltechnologies/assets/perspectives/2030/pdf/Realizing-2030-A-Divided-Vision-of-the-Future-Summary.pdf.

† https://www.nimh.nih.gov/health/statistics/major-depression.shtml#part_155029.

‡ https://adaa.org/about-adaa/press-room/facts-statistics#:~:text=The%20leading%20cause%20of%20disability,older%20in%20a%20given%20year.

§ https://www.pewsocialtrends.org/2019/02/20/most-u-s-teens-see-anxiety-and-depression-as-a-major-problem-among-their-peers/.

As human beings, we're wired with evolutionary instincts to survive. We continuously assess situations to determine risk and safety. Is this person a threat? Will this thing harm me? We usually adapt to survive. But given the accelerated rate of change in today's economy, we increasingly feel uncomfortable and unsafe. Fear and anxiety paralyze us.

What do we do? I believe we must learn to develop the proper mindset to confront uncertainty and ambiguity.

Mental health experts often employ a technique called cognitive behavioral therapy (CBT) to treat depression and anxiety. Specifically, CBT focuses on helping people identify unhelpful thoughts that may distort their reality and then develop practical solutions to challenge and overcome those distortions.

For example, a student fails a math test. The student tells himself that he is a failure and will never graduate from high school and go to college. Using CBT, a therapist trains the student not to focus on one test but rather on his entire body of work, including good grades in English and history and success in extracurricular activities. The therapist might have the student craft a résumé so he can better visualize his achievements.

In effect, CBT enables people to rewire their brains to reframe an unpleasant situation in a way that relieves the depression and anxiety it causes.

Throughout my career, we have often used a CBT type of approach to help managers who were struggling with motivation or having a case of the blues. For example, we would send them on a college recruiting visit or to the next job fair, and they almost always came back refreshed and energized.

Why? They got to take a breath and regain perspective by talking to people who did not work at the company. College recruiting trips exposed them to people who were full of energy and excited about the prospect of working. And in the course of these visits, our managers spent all day sharing and talking about all the good things the company offers—benefits, perks, compelling work—and in doing so, they reminded themselves why they began working at the company in the first place. These recruiting trips provided our leaders with time to step back and get a new perspective. Did it work all the time? No. But more times than not, this was an excellent booster for people who were feeling out of sorts.

Mental health is not trivial, and in recent years addressing this has even become a big industry. Recently, *The Atlantic* labeled this industry the "Anxiety Economy,"* and a company by the name of Calm that developed a meditation app has become the first unicorn in this fast-emerging industry.†

REFRAMING ENTREPRENEUR

In 2015 Muhammad Yunus visited San Francisco and met an adoring crowd of start-up employees. Yunus is perhaps best known for being the founder of the microfinance movement, for which he won the Nobel Peace Prize. His organization, Grameen Bank, lends small amounts of money to entrepreneurs in developing countries.

Yunus is a disruptor in the realest sense. He not only challenges how banks make money but also our assumptions about work in general.

---

* https://www.theatlantic.com/business/archive/2012/05/the-anxiety-economy-why-the-future-of-work-will-be-all-about-stress/256794/.

† https://www.fastcompany.com/90302858/calm-just-became-the-first-meditation-unicorn-with-its-88m-series-b.

"It's the tyranny of employment," Yunus said at the time. "Who said we have to be workers? They're telling our children as we send them to school, 'Work hard so you can get a good job.' The teachers are telling them, 'Work hard, get a good job. If you don't get a job, you are a failure.'

"You go to college, and you come out with a certificate that employers value," he continued. "All the pride and everything is getting a good job. That's all."

We tend to associate entrepreneurialism with people who start companies. But what if we're taking too narrow of a view of that concept? Who says you have to start a company to be an entrepreneur?

Let's start with the fact that you're reading this book. You have recognized a problem and chosen to collect data, which already places you ahead of the class. You're demonstrating the kind of qualities employers increasingly demand today. In an economy that's hard to predict, employers want people with "soft skills" such as problem-solving and the ability to embrace change, accept new information, and respond accordingly. The best competitive advantage you can develop is the capacity to grow, learn, and adapt so that regardless of how the markets change or how technology changes, you will be prepared to succeed. While that may sound overly obvious or trite, I cannot overstate this point.

As it turns out, ambiguity is not an obstacle but rather a highly marketable job skill.

"Due to this growing ambiguity in organizations, it follows that those who can *tolerate* or even *embrace* ambiguity at work will be well placed to perform well in contemporary organizations," said researchers who conducted a 2018 study at the Queensland University of Technology in Brisbane, Australia.

While there is a vast body of research to support the link between the so-called "tolerance of ambiguity" (TOA) and general traits like leadership and creativity, the Queensland study sought to establish connections between TOA and more contextualized workplace situations.

Through a series of online surveys, the researchers found TOA significantly predicted income and resilience. The study also placed a high value on how well employees could manage uncertainty.

The best competitive advantage you can develop is the ongoing capacity to grow, learn, and adapt so that regardless of how the markets change or how technology changes, you will be prepared to succeed.

"We believe that Managing the Uncertainty is an important dimension . . . because it allows individuals high in TOA to excel in ambiguous situations," the researchers wrote. "In order for employees to be able to achieve their goals, they need to effectively navigate through ambiguous situations.

"Indeed, there were a number of positive outcomes that were more likely to be displayed by people with high levels of Managing the Uncertainty. These included being task focused and goal oriented, being effective in teams, and displaying high levels of conscientiousness."

The study also mentioned something I found particularly interesting: a strong relationship between TOA and "entrepreneurial intentions."

Employees who displayed strong entrepreneurial intentions not only tolerated ambiguity well but actively sought it out by consistently challenging themselves. Those employees tended to perform exceptionally well at their jobs.

"The inclination to seek out challenging work and ultimately create uncertainty was strongly associated with a range of positive work outcomes," the study said.

You might not be running a business in a traditional sense, but you are certainly running the business of you.* And to run that business well, you need to adopt an entrepreneur's mindset:

- Where others see ambiguity, you see a chance to distinguish yourself.
- Where other people see problems, you see opportunities.
- Where others see technology eliminating jobs, you see new ways of creating value or new sources of revenue.

CREATING VALUE MAKES YOU MORE VALUABLE

Not long ago I was hanging out with my sons and discovered they were watching a young man named Zach Hample on You-Tube. Hample filmed himself catching baseballs at stadiums around the world.

Amazingly, on that premise alone, he built a following of close to five hundred thousand people, and many of his videos attracted over one million views. My boys thought Zach was a god. "Look, Dad! He has millions of viewers, and he is making a ton of money doing that."

---

* In 2012, Reid Hoffman and Ben Casnocha published The Start-Up of YOU, which is a treasure trove of great ideas on how to adapt to the future and how to transform your career. As part of this, they built a website filled with resources, videos, and interviews.

Listening to my boys, I realized YouTube might offer them a viable career path. Here was a guy who had built a business doing something that did not even exist a decade ago.

| *Do stuff that matters to others, and you will be rewarded.*

Did Hample set out to be a YouTuber? Probably not. He did something he loved, shared it with the world, and discovered a new career path. That's the appeal of the new economy: someone can find a way to make a living doing something they enjoy and that defies the traditional definition of a job or working for a company. Like Hample, there are plenty of people who use eBay, Craigslist, YouTube, or other platforms to build a new career or to supplement a current one. And these new options seem to have sprouted out of nowhere.*

Hample offered an excellent lesson for my boys: regardless of your job, do stuff that matters to others, and you will be rewarded.

A few months later, we were on vacation in Southern California and decided to attend an Angels-versus-Brewers baseball game. We were determined to see if we could replicate what we had learned watching Hample's YouTube videos. The boys did their homework; they examined the ballpark's dimensions to

---

* We still are learning what this new gig economy means and how it will impact the future of work. We see that it is offering many new choices and options to supplement incomes or in some cases to create whole new career paths. In the United States, the system of health care is built to support having a job and working for an employer. Affordable health care for people who work gig jobs full time is still remote. Further, many important laws and regulations in the United States and other countries still are designed for people to work for an employer. For example, trying to get a home loan when you are a gig worker is extremely difficult. There are many barriers like these blocking the proliferation of gig workers in the United States and many countries. For more on the gig economy, go here: https://www.nytimes.com/2019/09/15/upshot/gig-economy-limits-labor-market-uber-california.html.

figure out the best location where they could catch a baseball, and they researched what times the gates opened and how long batting practice took place. They tried to determine the best place for us to station ourselves to catch the most baseballs. We arrived at the park thirty minutes before the gates opened, and we all had our baseball gloves. We were ready!

Now, to be honest, in my life I have attended nearly one hundred games over many years, and I've never caught a baseball at a game. Not even once! So, I did not hold out much hope for our venture, but I was not going to spoil the mojo with my sons. My fears of failure faded quickly. Within the first fifteen minutes, my twins each collected three baseballs. By the end of the game, we collectively had thirteen baseballs!

I was in shock, and their smiles were too big to measure. At one point we started to give our balls to other kids since we were embarrassed by how many we had collected. We took home eight balls that night, and our faith in this new economy took deeper root. We did not film ourselves like Zach did, but the point was made, and we all learned a big lesson.

WE ARE ALL ENTREPRENEURS

In a dynamic economy, employees must adopt similar entrepreneurial traits toward their livelihoods, including resourcefulness, personal branding, and strategic thinking.

We all need to embrace experimentation in the same manner as Zach Hample and stage actors. We need to consider how we can build content that matters. It's not always rocket science. Hample needed just a smart phone and an internet connection to start his business.

During his visit to San Francisco, Muhammed Yunus criticized an economic system that artificially divides people into workers and entrepreneurs. In his view, everyone, not just a select few who happen to have access to financial capital, is an entrepreneur.

"Some people tell me, 'Not all human beings are entrepreneurs,'" Yunus said. "'Some have that capability. Others do not have that capability.' I say, 'Why do you say that? You distort them to make them workers.'"

> *In a dynamic economy, employees must adopt similar entrepreneurial traits toward their livelihoods, including resourcefulness, personal branding, and strategic thinking.*

Mohanjit Jolly is a successful venture capitalist and board member in Palo Alto, California. He graduated from MIT and UCLA's Anderson School of Management. As a founding partner of Iron Pillar, he has invested in dozens of companies, mostly start-ups, in India and the United States. He is continually surrounded by start-up entrepreneurs.

While Jolly holds great passion for technology, he will be the first to tell you that success or failure always comes down to people.

"When I invest, the first thing I look for is the self-awareness quotient of the entrepreneur, founder, or CEO," he told me. "Do they know what they know, and do they know what they do not know? Do they have the capability of not only identifying the gap but also having the resourcefulness to fill that gap with people and advisors in their network who can help them?

"I also want to know if they have an infectious passion that they can make go viral and be able to attract the best and brightest," he said.

As a seasoned investor, Jolly knows that leaders will continuously face new challenges, so the more capable they are of dealing with inevitable adversity, the more likely they will be to succeed. Employees should adopt the same mindset: expect the unexpected challenges and build the abilities to address the unknown through mentors, coaches, and networks.

This is an excellent lesson for all of us to think about when we look at the future of work. In a world where we are increasingly facing new challenges, new technology, and new processes, our success will derive from how we tackle new things that inevitably come our way. We should expect these challenges and focus on building our ability to confront them.

> *In a world where we are increasingly facing new challenges, new technology, and new processes, our success will derive from how we tackle new things that inevitably come our way.*

Sometimes we are led to believe that entrepreneurs are people who are highly innovative, and in so doing we think of how they build new products. I used to think entrepreneurs were a different breed. That is not true. Being an entrepreneur does not require that you start a company. However, it just so happens if you do want to start a company, it's easier than ever.* While that is true, what is significantly more critical, as Jolly has told us, is that the ability to be self-aware and to be highly focused on filling the gaps of unknown areas will allow us to find innovations in our own

---

* https://www.businessinsider.com/why-now-is-the-best-time-to-start-a-company-2014-10.

ways. Entrepreneurs are people who creatively adapt to shifting circumstances. We can all be entrepreneurs in that sense, and our value is built by the people we surround ourselves with, people who help us, mentor and coach us, and offer insights and ideas when we hit an inevitable gap of the unknown.

> *Entrepreneurs are people who creatively adapt to shifting circumstances.*

HUMANITY IS MORE IMPORTANT THAN EVER

Technological disruption is not going to slow down anytime soon. We are going to find ourselves in new, ambiguous situations increasingly.

For example, we're inundated with stories about robots stealing our jobs. We are seeing more and more articles where authors are making a distinction between "human employees"* and other forms of employees. Human employees? I never thought we needed to make that distinction.

But we enjoy one significant advantage: we are human. Even with all of our frailty, fears, and insecurities, our humanity has never been more critical in the job market. Why? We can adapt.

Take the travel industry.

Before the internet, people used travel agents to book trips. Once people could book travel online, 90 percent of travel agents were out of work. You could assume the story would end there.

But companies like Expedia, Priceline, Trip Advisor, Kayak,

---

* https://www.hrtechnologist.com/articles/digital-transformation/advancements-in-ai-and-its-impact-on-human-employees/.

and Yelp soon emerged. The internet generated far more new jobs than the number of travel agents it displaced.

In his blog post, "What it Really Means to Humanize Work," Tim Leberecht writes, "Humans . . . will only thrive if we keep investing in what makes us inherently human: vulnerability, empathy, intuition, emotion, and imagination." Leberecht makes a great point, and this is highly encouraging for those of us who see robots, AI, and automation in our career rearview mirrors.*

> *We will only thrive if we keep investing in what makes us inherently human: vulnerability, empathy, intuition, emotion, and imagination.*
>
> —Tim Leberecht

We are all improv actors today, waiting for the scene to materialize in our unpredictable world of work. And when it does, we must react fast, think creatively, and engage with whatever situation life thrusts upon us. We can move forward with the confidence of knowing that our human abilities are most in demand by CEOs today. It's up to us to invest in ourselves.

The show must go on.

---

* https://www.workhuman.com/resources/globoforce-blog/what-it-really-means-to-humanize-work#:~:text=Humans%20may%20survive%20robots%20at,feel%E2%80%94and%20feel%20for%20others.

2

TOWARD A LEARNING MINDSET

DON'T BE HOMER SIMPSON

A teacher glumly walks into a classroom at the adult education center.

"Welcome to Remedial Science One-A," he says. "My wife recently passed away. I thought teaching might ease my loneliness."

"Will this be on the test?" a man in the front row asks.

"No!" the teacher says.

"Ohhh . . ." the man says. He quickly erases what he wrote on his notepad: "DEAD WIFE."

In many ways, Homer Simpson, the patriarch of the animated TV series *The Simpsons*, personifies how we have come to see education over the years. Students care more about "What do I need to memorize to pass the test?" than "What can I learn to achieve future success?" For many students, the test itself seems more important than the overall lesson itself.

When it comes to education, we live in an unusual paradox. A college degree is more imperative than ever: data shows college graduates earn higher incomes than people who lack a degree. However, in the United States, student loan debt stands at a staggering $1.5 trillion and counting. Faced with deep debt, rapid economic changes, and out-of-date curricula, some people are questioning the value of going to college at all.

Our education system is increasingly failing to prepare students for the challenges of a changing, dynamic economy. Instead of teaching students how to problem solve in the face of ambiguity and failure, schools have continued to repeat information to students and test them on how well they can recall that information.

As a longtime recruiter, I know employers want people who can communicate well and adapt quickly to shifting circumstances. Employees who graduate from education systems that simply train them to memorize information will find it hard to compete in the twenty-first-century economy.

> *We need to think about formal education as an exercise to grow our ability to learn more new things and apply them quickly versus an activity to land a job.*

Most importantly, we need to stop thinking that people stop learning after they complete college or that high school is simply a means to get to college. Society has lulled us into a false belief that a college degree is the only gateway to a good career or that it automatically guarantees people financial and professional security. That we no longer need to acquire new skills or improve our existing set. That intellectual curiosity is a luxury many of us can't afford.

Nothing could be further from the truth.

We need to think about formal education as an exercise to grow our ability to learn more new things and apply them quickly versus an activity to land a job.

John Seely Brown is a former chief scientist and CEO of Xerox PARC. In its heyday, Xerox was a great place for innovation, having spawned many new technologies, including laser printers and the graphic user interface, a feature that Apple founder Steve Jobs used for the Mac computer.

In his book *A New Culture of Learning*, Brown estimates the half-life of a skill today at only *five years*. The figure, if correct, means most of what you learn in school will be irrelevant after a decade at most.

"Our desire to learn should always be active and constant," Brown said. We should look at our daily activities, whether at home or the office, as opportunities to continually explore, learn, and grow.

In other words, people need to develop a proactive, take-charge approach to education and training that extends into everyday life, not just the classroom or office.

> *Your ability to learn skills, not the skills themselves, will allow you to weather any career change. This is the ultimate career insurance.*

"On the employee side, the data continues to reveal that people want to grow and develop above all else," Sally Thornton, CEO of Forshay, told me. "Doubling down on learning and creativity is essential because that's the stuff that will remain true and important in the future of work. What makes someone look great today is that they're stretching themselves."

People tend to ask Thornton about the magic elixir of skills they need to stay relevant in the job market. Should I know Java or some other programming language? Should I go to block-chain boot camp or earn an online microdegree? Should I study digital marketing?

All of these options can't hurt. But as Seely Brown previously told us, skills, particularly technical skills, don't age well. So why should we chase something that may become obsolete not long after we learn it? In truth, there are no specific skills that will fully protect you from disruption.

> *However, your ability to learn skills, not the skills themselves, will allow you to weather any career change. That's the ultimate career insurance.*

"In this fluid future of work, we have to say, 'How am I learning and growing? What sparks me?'" Thornton said. "And so this learning mindset and growth mindset will serve people the best."

DIMINISHING RETURNS

College continues to occupy a prominent place in American culture.

Middle-class professions that once didn't require a college degree now increasingly do. Of the 270 occupations in the United States tracked by *The Economist*, all but nine occupations have seen the number of college-educated employees rise.* For example, in 1970 only 16 percent of registered nurses held a bach-

---

*   https://www.economist.com/graphic-detail/2018/02/01/the-economic-re-
turns-to-university.

elor's degree, compared to 60 percent in 2015.

Yet employees are finding it increasingly hard to stand out because technology allows people access to the same information around the world.

"It used to be that access to education was scarce," David Blake, co-founder of Degreed and author of *The Expertise Economy*, wrote.*

"In that world, universities and employers had a specific role to play—to gather information and administer education and skill development programs. But now information and education are abundant wherever people have access to the internet. That makes skill development available at any time on any day, which makes the process of continuous learning a standard business expectation."

But college graduates see diminishing returns on their massive investments. *The Economist* estimates that more than half of the professions whose employees attended college since 1970 have seen *real wages decline.*† As a college graduate, you probably will earn more than a high school graduate, but that doesn't mean you can expect to get a raise.

The lack of wage gains is troubling, especially since the United States has enjoyed strong economic growth and a tight labor market over the past several years. One big reason for the stagnation, economists say, is the lack of productivity growth. Employees may be better educated, at least on paper, but they are not necessarily more productive.

---

* https://www.thenational.ae/business/why-skills-are-the-currency-of-the-future-of-work-1.849310.

† https://www.economist.com/graphic-detail/2018/02/01/the-economic-returns-to-university.

Why is that? Perhaps higher education is not providing employees the skills and mindset they need to compete in a twenty-first-century economy that requires adaptation and improvisation.

"Graduates are confronted with a labor market that increasingly puts a premium on creativity, exploring uncertainties, and learning from failure," author Jamie Holmes writes, "yet many college professors still act like old-school golf instructors focused on automatically applying skills, rather than helping students learn to deal with the challenges of invention."*

Holmes argues that colleges should teach students not only how to succeed but also how to fail. Failure, he said, teaches resilience to students who think they can find a clear answer to every problem.

> *Graduates are confronted with a labor market that increasingly puts a premium on creativity, exploring uncertainties, and learning from failure, yet many college professors still act like old-school golf instructors focused on automatically applying skills.*
>
> —Jamie Holmes

"Traditional lecturing . . . encourages an approach increasingly at odds with the challenges graduates face," Holmes writes. "Have you ever had a lecturer highlight the necessity of stumbling, errors, and luck in developing breakthrough innovations? Have you ever been given a classroom assignment that you were 80 percent likely to fail at, matching an entrepreneur's odds?

---

*   Jamie Holmes, *Nonsense* (New York: Broadway Books, 2015), 165.

Have you ever confronted a problem that has no solution? Have you practiced overcoming how it feels to fail?"*

In his book *The End of Average*, Harvard graduate school professor Todd Rose argues schools pigeonhole kids into categories based on limited criteria like grades and test scores. Schools need to take account of each kid's strengths and weaknesses. Rose himself represents a fantastic story of resilience and agility. A high school dropout who spent time on welfare and had almost a dozen minimum wage jobs, a husband, and a father all before he was twenty years old, Rose has a unique and compelling point of view around rethinking education and preparing ourselves for the future.

"At the end of the day, it's about having more flexibility in design, so we're not just locking kids out because of their individuality unnecessarily," Rose wrote. "When schools aren't responsive to them as individuals, the students don't know who they are, and the teacher has the wrong lens to think about the kids, and we're all constrained by these narrow metrics of success.

"We need to be more competency based," he continued. "I don't care how you compare to the student next to you. I want to know whether you are mastering the things you need to master. Grades, for example, are too one-dimensional. You cannot collapse what a student knows or is capable of knowing or doing into a letter."

From the perspective of building a compelling career, Rose gives us some outstanding guidance here. Find *your* path, and recognize what makes you unique and how you can build upon that to unlock your full potential.

Given these factors and the explosion of alternative schools

---

*   Holmes, 166.

like Coursera, Lynda.com, massive open online courses (MOOCs), Singularity, and Udacity, traditional universities and colleges are starting to feel the pinch. The late Harvard University business professor Clayton Christensen predicts half of the four thousand schools in the United States will go bankrupt over the next few decades, and that was before COVID-19 kicked in.

Enrollment at business schools across the world is already declining.* In 2017 the University of Iowa said it plans to close its once top-ranked full-time MBA program. The University of Illinois at Urbana–Champaign followed suit.†

Students are increasingly unwilling to disconnect themselves from the job market for two years to earn a degree, especially when their peers, in Silicon Valley in particular, are already launching businesses.

"Young people today are seeing people just like them going out, starting, and building incredibly successful companies," said David Hensley, director of the John Pappajohn Entrepreneurial Center at the University of Iowa.‡

A growing number of prominent companies are looking for other ways to evaluate talent without relying so much on college credentials.§

Even the revered Google, known for its early focus on only

---

* https://www.washingtonpost.com/education/2018/10/07/mba-enrollment-is-down-again-whats-future-degree/?utm_term=.b779ae4a573f.

† https://www.thegazette.com/subject/news/education/university-of-iowa-graduates-last-full-time-mba-class-tippie-college-of-business-masters-of-business-administration-20190510.

‡ https://www.thegazette.com/subject/news/education/university-of-iowa-graduates-last-full-time-mba-class-tippie-college-of-business-masters-of-business-administration-20190510.

§ https://www.cnbc.com/2018/08/16/15-companies-that-no-longer-require-employees-to-have-a-college-degree.html.

hiring the best talent with the best grades from the best schools, learned after they took a long, in-depth look at their data that there was no correlation between their top talent and the GPA they had in school or whether or not they had gone to a "top-tier" university. In a lengthy *New York Times* article published in 2013, Laslo Bock, then head of HR, said, "One of the things we've seen from all our data crunching is that GPAs are worthless as a criterion for hiring, and test scores are worthless—no correlation at all, except for brand-new college grads, where there's a slight correlation. Google famously used to ask everyone for a transcript and GPAs and test scores, but we don't anymore, unless you're just a few years out of school. We found that they don't predict anything."*

Bock went on to mention that after this research, Google began to hire many employees who had never even gone to college.

Recently Apple, IBM, Tesla, Costco, Chipotle, Whole Foods, and Hilton joined the list of companies who no longer require a four-year degree.†

MIMI GIGOUX AND THE POWER OF NO COLLEGE DEGREE

My career was massively changed by working for someone who never went to college. Mimi Gigoux started her career as a receptionist after finishing high school and went on to become one of the top human resources executives in Silicon Valley at

---

Cisco Systems. Despite not having gone to college, over the years Mimi, who was naturally very bright and curious, developed an uncanny ability to identify people's true motivations and aspirations. She couldn't care less where you went to school or what fancy company you may have worked for—she went right to your heart and mind and focused on learning who *you* were. This allowed her to see things in people and to lead teams in amazingly successful ways. Mimi was a force of positive energy whose way of thinking was not cluttered by a college education that might have predisposed her to believe she had to think or act in specific ways. Mimi always lit up the room, and knowing she did not have a degree may have led her to sharpen and rely on her natural abilities.

Mimi hired me in 1998 to join her M&A acquisition integration team at Cisco, which at the time was a fast-growing and very hot company in Silicon Valley. While I was excited that Mimi had hired me, I doubt anyone other than Mimi would have hired me for that job because I had zero M&A experience. Zero. But Mimi saw something in me that even I didn't see. Somehow she knew I would love M&A work and that I'd be good at it.

Boy, was she right. I *loved* it. Mimi went on to be written up in the *Wall Street Journal** for building Cisco's world-class M&A team, and inside the company she was known to be one of the company's best negotiators. That's right, a high school graduate with no college degree who started out as a secretary rose to be recognized by the *Wall Street Journal* for exceptional performance in arguably the most complex change event a company could ever experience: being acquired by another company!

---

*   https://www.wsj.com/articles/SB95187454498765678.

> *College is no longer the investment that will guarantee us a viable career path.*

Working for Mimi taught me many things, such as: don't assume that someone who did not go to college is not amazingly talented, always try to hire people better than you, take the time to know people and understand them, and always encourage others to stretch and take on new challenges. Mimi might not have had a college degree, but she had a self-taught PhD in people and understanding how to bring out their best. Sadly, Mimi passed away suddenly a few years ago after complications from surgery.* Her legacy lives on in me, her children, and the many lives she touched. Lacking a college education did not impede Mimi's success. It may have enabled it.

CAPACITY TO LEARN TRUMPS WHERE YOU WENT TO SCHOOL

Ernst & Young (EY) is one of the most recognized accounting and professional services firms in the world, and recently, Cadie Thompson and Melia Russell published an article† in *Business Insider* that sheds more light on what employers are looking for today. EY hires hundreds of graduates every year, and one senior partner noted, "A college degree in a relevant field is no longer a requisite for hiring . . . Instead, the firm looks for continuous learners—people who show a desire to learn new skills . . . What

---

*   https://www.findagrave.com/memorial/152279799/marilyn-ann-gigoux.

†   https://www.businessinsider.com/how-to-get-hired-at-ey-ernst-young-2020-1?nr_email_referer=1&utm_source=Sailthru&utm_medium=email&utm_content=BIPrime_Strategy&utm_campaign=BI%20Prime%20-%20Strategy%202020-01-23&utm_term=BI%20Prime%20-%20Strategy%20Insider.

we're recognizing is that we may have some people who are deep specialists in product engineering, but actually we need a lot of people who have a broad understanding or a high-level understanding of what product engineering is or what AI can do or what blockchain can do . . . So that desire, and that willingness to do that, is incredibly important."

In the article the EY senior partner goes so far as to say that an individual's desire to learn may not even "manifest itself through a university degree. That's why we are less focused on the academics, and we're more focused on what's the attitude to learning."

> *An individual's desire to learn may not even "manifest itself through a university degree. That's why we are less focused on the academics, and we're more focused on what's the attitude to learning."*

EY's main focus today is to help hundreds of global companies digitally transform. In other words, they have a front-row seat to determine what skills are most in demand and most needed as companies strive to compete in the future. Their conclusion? The essential skill for tomorrow is your capacity to learn, and this is more important to them than where you went to school or even *if* you went to school.

I'm not suggesting college degrees are worthless. As the recent examples of parents cheating and breaking laws to get their kids into high-profile universities suggest[*], many of us still believe a college experience is necessary for a successful life. But is college still an investment that will guarantee us a

---

[*]   https://www.cnn.com/2019/03/13/us/parents-college-admission-cheating-scandal/index.html.

viable career path? Perhaps we should see college as part of the ongoing process of self-improvement, not the end goal.

The good news is, affordable education and training are already within your grasp. Beyond the massive increase in access to free education, many employers today offer substantial help with tuition reimbursement. Two companies (AMD and Cisco) fully paid for my master's degree in organization development at the University of San Francisco through tuition reimbursement.

According to a 2018 survey by WorldatWork and recruitment firm Korn Ferry,* 85 percent of companies said they offered employees tuition reimbursement, and nearly 20 percent said they provided tuition discounts.

For employers, paying for employees' education is no simple matter. Some employers are reluctant to fully support degree programs for their employees, fearing this will simply make their employees more attractive for competitors to steal. Or perhaps employees will demand more compensation if they complete a certificate or a degree.

In the end, the benefits far outweigh the risks. An old parable goes something like this: A CFO and a CEO are talking about employee development. The CFO says to the CEO, "Wow, developing our employees is costing us a lot of money!" to which the CEO replies, "What is the cost if we don't develop our employees?"

"It is something of a surprise that any employers should offer such support, let alone that most employers do," Peter Capelli, a professor of management at the University of Pennsylvania's Wharton School, wrote in a paper published by the National Bureau of Economic Research.†

---

*   https://www.worldatwork.org/dA/f2b21babd0/total-rewards-incentive-survey-2018-new.pdf.

†   https://www.nber.org/papers/w9225.pdf.

But the tight job market and shortage of talent have convinced many employers that they must invest in their workforce and try to retain their best employees, which lowers costs.

"Workers who use tuition assistance have productivity that is above market levels," Capelli wrote. "Turnover is lower ... and that result seems consistent with the view that staff stay with firms longer to make full use of tuition assistance plans. Lower turnover in itself is a source of cost savings for employers by reducing search and hiring costs."* Companies that invest in growing, reskilling, and continually developing their staff realize many benefits.

CHIPOTLE'S ENLIGHTENED DEVELOPMENT

Chipotle has a very progressive view of talent development and investments in learning. As an organization with twenty-five hundred-plus restaurants and over eighty thousand employees, having a leading people strategy is essential. As Marissa Andrada, Chipotle's chief people officer, says, "It all begins with the recognition that innovation will come from their people, so investing in making their people better is a no-brainer."†

Chipotle's tuition reimbursement not only covers two-year and four-year degrees, but it also includes certificate and credential programs as well as trade schools and English as a Second Language (ESL) classes. Chipotle will even reimburse students for completing their high school diploma, not just for the

---

* https://www.nber.org/papers/w9225.pdf.

† https://thefutureoflearninganddevelopment.libsyn.com/3-using-ld-to-attract-retain-talent-with-marissa-andrada-chief-people-officer-at-chipotle.

employees, but for anyone in their family. As Andrada states, "We believe if you are going through this process, you need the support network at home." In 2019 Chipotle took their progressive approach a step further and announced a relationship with six universities wherein Chipotle will pay for 100 percent of your schooling as long as you have worked there at least 120 days for fifteen hours a week. No strings attached. No requirement to stay after you finish school. And no cap on the cost! Finding an organization that offers this depth of educational support with no strings attached is rare, and Chipotle is an enlightened leader in this regard.

> *We want them to stick around after the degree . . . but if they discover a passion, we want them to go pursue that.*
> —Marissa Andrada, chief people officer, Chipotle

When Andrada was asked if Chipotle worries about people leaving once they earn a degree, she said, "We want them to stick around after the degree . . . but if they discover a passion, we want them to go pursue that." Chipotle's approach is an example of how companies can think differently about talent development. This approach takes the long view of the relationship, and it's honest, too. It recognizes that people change and may discover new passions and interests, but that does not prevent them from investing in employee development.

The majority of employers today offer employees additional training and development benefits, the WorldatWork and Korn Ferry survey says, including formal coaching and mentoring (52 percent), leadership training (85 percent), outside seminars/conferences (93 percent), and classroom/virtual learning (92 percent).

Over the past decade, the nontraditional education sector has rapidly grown to a billion-dollar market. We have witnessed the emergence of organizations like Coursera and edX, which offer free online classes from venerable institutions like Harvard, MIT, Microsoft, and the Smithsonian. These MOOCs also grant students certifications and degrees on everything from software coding and marketing to languages and genetics.

We must embrace lifelong learning as a necessity, not a luxury. This notion of the need to always be learning and growing is not new. Several professions require members to refresh their skills regularly. Lawyers and public accountants must take several classes every year to preserve their credentials. The same goes for Realtors, doctors, and nurses. Every employee should consider adopting this mindset.

LEARNING AGILITY AND GROWTH MINDSET

Kelly Palmer is chief learning officer at educational technology firm Degreed and has designed world-class training and development platforms at Sun Microsystems, Yahoo, and LinkedIn.

Palmer recently told me the most important skill people need to develop is something she calls "learning agility." "Learning agility is having the curiosity and motivation to learn new things throughout the entirety of your career. Gone are the days where a four-year degree will give you all the knowledge you need to stay competitive in your professional careers."[*]

---

[*] Another great definition of learning agility comes from Abhishek Jha: "Learning agility is knowing what to do when you don't know what to do." https://www.disprz.com/blog/what-is-learning-agility/. Jha says people who are "learning agile":

> *People need to demonstrate intent and purpose in learning new information versus waiting for someone else to spoon-feed ideas to them.*

In *The Expertise Economy*, a book Palmer cowrote with David Blake, the duo argue we should always be pursuing development opportunities.* "Innovation means pushing beyond the status quo," they said. "You have to go where others haven't been, which necessitates you know how to learn and skill yourself. All of the very best innovators have been great lifelong, self-directed learners—Bill Gates, Elon Musk, and Clayton Christensen are all on the record as having read the entire encyclopedia as children."†

> *Lifelong learning is not about being in a classroom for the rest of your life so much as it means being in a constant state of curiosity about your environment and circumstances and regularly seeking to understand and develop.*

- Constantly look out for new experiences to learn from
- Thrive on complex problems and challenges
- Enjoy making sense out of the different experiences they encounter
- Deliver better performance as they have new skills ingrained in them

* When I advise friends, families, and clients about the ideal attributes of a new employer, commitment to your learning velocity and your development are at the top the list. I advise them to ask:
  - Have they designed work in such a way that my experiences will allow me to grow and build my network?
  - Do they allow me to move around to different departments to face new challenges and assignments?
  - Do they see their managers as coaches and mentors?
  - Do I see people moving inside the organization?
  - Do I see the people who have left the company doing interesting things?
  - Do they support me taking risks and learning from my mistakes?

† https://www.thenational.ae/business/why-skills-are-the-currency-of-the-future-of-work-1.849310.

While reading a whole encyclopedia may seem extreme, it does show a massive innate curiosity, and that curiosity can manifest itself in many different ways. Lifelong learning is not about being in a classroom for the rest of your life as much as being in a constant state of curiosity about your environment and circumstances and regularly seeking to understand and develop.

> *Ultimately, the most valuable asset you can possess as an employee is something that you can't necessarily teach: curiosity.*

Ultimately, the most valuable asset you can possess as an employee is something that you can't necessarily teach: curiosity.

And this leads us to a crucial mindset for employees today, a term coined by Carol Dweck in 2003 as the "growth mindset." In 2003 Dweck was studying students' mindsets and in her work discovered that how students perceived their abilities played a crucial role in their motivation and achievement: "We found that if we changed students' mindsets, we could boost their achievement. More precisely, students who believed their intelligence could be developed (a growth mindset) outperformed those who believed their intelligence was fixed (a fixed mindset). And when students learned through a structured program that they could grow their brains and increase their intellectual abilities, they did better. Finally, we found that having children focus on the process that leads to learning (like hard work or trying new strategies) could foster a growth mindset and its benefits."*

---

*   https://www.edweek.org/ew/articles/2015/09/23/carol-dweck-revisits-the-growth-mindset.html?cmp=cpc-goog-ew-growth+mindset&ccid=growth+mindset&c-cag=growth+mindset&cckw=%2Bgrowth%20%2Bmindset&cccv=content+ad&g-

Learning agility and having a growth mindset are closely tied and necessary in a world where the skills we need seem to change faster than ever, and our need to learn new stuff is rising. "In a growth mindset, people believe that their most basic abilities can be developed through dedication and hard work—brains and talent are just the starting point. This view creates a love of learning and a resilience that is essential for great accomplishment."

> *In a growth mindset, people believe that their most basic abilities can be developed through dedication and hard work— brains and talent are just the starting point. This view creates a love of learning and a resilience that is essential for great accomplishment.*
>
> —Carol Dweck, author and researcher

Clearly, in today's world of work, leveraging your growth mindset is a necessary strategy for a life requiring more learning and change.* If you believe you can learn, you have a considerable advantage. This does not mean learning will always be easy or fun, but we both know it's necessary for success today. And listen, the best part about this is that it's just a choice of how we want to frame learning. If you prefer to say to yourself, "I'm not good at _____ (math, software, computers . . . fill in the blank), it's not my thing," you are limiting yourself. If instead you say, "I'm not good at _____ *yet*," you are bringing out your growth mindset.

---

clid=CjoKEQiAnvfDBRCXrabLl6-6t-0BEiQAW4SRUM7nekFn0Txc675qBMSJycF-gwERohguZWVmNDcSUg5gaAk3I8P8HAQ.

*   For more information on the growth mindset: https://hbr.org/2016/01/what-having-a-growth-mindset-actually-means.

Dweck also tells us that "the feeling of something new that we are learning being hard is the feeling of your brain growing!" We must believe we can learn new things, that we can adapt, and this belief will diminish our fears, allow us to learn new things, again and again, and ultimately set us up for career success. It's not always easy, but it's necessary.

BUILDING SKILLS AND CAREER PATHS OUTSIDE OF WORK

Learning can take many forms. Sometimes our hobbies and special interests are not just sources of inspiration but also catalysts for real career opportunities. Not all hobbies and personal interests directly translate into applicable job skills. But many do, often in the most unexpected ways.

Arielle Lapiano, a public relations executive at Paul Hastings law firm in New York, is a lifelong learner.

"I am just innately somebody who is always interested in a lot of different things, and I want to fuel that interest," Lapiano, a married mother of two, told me. "I don't do it explicitly to have any big benefit. However, that being said, I think that learning a new skill, taking up a new hobby, helps you in numerous different ways that are always surprising."

For example, Lapiano is an avid ballroom dancer and has participated in several competitions.

"I got into dancing a while ago because I just thought it was a fun, different thing to do," she said. "I would credit dancing for helping to prepare me to be a better presenter at work. Part of my job is occasionally doing presentations to the team, and sometimes doing presentations for clients. I don't know that I would have the confidence to be able to stand up in front of a room to do that had I not actually had the experience of being a dancer."

Lapiano takes the long view of her career that all of the pieces have added up to the whole. I could not agree more. This is a much healthier perspective than the one that believes that to be good in business you have to major in business or study business in school. This is not necessarily true, and a LinkedIn study proved it.* Sometimes it's the diversity of experiences in life and at work that add to the depth you can bring to a job or career.†

"I sometimes have joked that my résumé looks a little bit like a collage," Lapiano said. "That the different pieces didn't necessarily suggest a great career path, or at least, like, a logical career path. But I enjoyed every different thing that I did, and

---

* https://www.linkedin.com/pulse/why-undergraduate-business-major-waste-time-money-jeff-selingo/.

† For years I took grief from people for being a history major in college. Honestly, in college I had no clue what I wanted to do with my life. I chose history because I was more curious about that topic than about anything else I had studied. I had no idea at the time how valuable my choice would become and how well it would serve me—and still serves me today. My liberal arts education taught me how to think critically, how to express myself, how to always question things and never make assumptions. It taught me to be in a constant state of curiosity and that there are patterns in life that sometimes the naked eye cannot see. My father was a minister, and my mother was highly engaged in the community, as well as a day care consultant. I had no role models in business in my family. Going into the business world felt like an adventure worth exploring, so I pursued that path and have realized some great experiences thankfully. In my thirty-plus years of working, I believe my history degree and liberal arts college experience prepared me well to face the biggest problems most organizations face—misunderstandings and miscommunications. In my first job out of college, I was a collector in the credit department of Esprit. After I was in that job a few months, they asked me to rewrite their entire process handbook because they could see I could communicate well. I was the youngest person in the department. Most of my colleagues were in their forties and had been doing the job for years. Yet they still chose me to undertake the task of rewriting the complex policy manual in a way that others could understand.

every job that I did got me to where I am today, which I think is amazing."

Volunteer and community work can also lead to some compelling learning and career options. Many of us spend time helping our communities, whether in schools, homeless shelters, or churches. Though altruistic, this work can also provide opportunities to build skills and professional networks.

Scott Lohmann is an excellent example of how being a volunteer can significantly alter one's career path. Lohmann has been a very distinguished sales executive in several major firms throughout his thirty-plus-year career for companies such as Entertainment Publications and Groupon.

Along with raising a family and maintaining a busy career, Lohmann still finds time to volunteer, whether for a public school, youth sports program, or organization raising money for first-generation college-bound teens. I met him while we were both volunteering as youth sports coaches. Lohmann also invested considerable time volunteering in development work— planning large fundraising events and helping to build sustainable giving plans. Lohman likes this work, and he is really good at it. These volunteer experiences served to help him develop new skills and apply some he already had. In a way, they were also a "career laboratory" in which he was able to experiment and see how much he liked this kind of work compared to his day jobs.

> *These volunteer experiences were also a "career laboratory" in which he was able to experiment and see how much he liked this kind of work compared to his day jobs.*

A few years ago, Lohman's passion for working in nonprofits grew so much that he decided to make what some might think is a significant career change. After networking with some friends, Lohmann joined the nonprofit firm VolunteerMatch full time as vice president of sales and marketing. VolunteerMatch connects professionals who want to volunteer with nonprofits. Scott had never worked full-time for a nonprofit before, and he was justifiably apprehensive, yet he took the leap.

At a time in life when most people might resist making such a significant change, Lohman decided to follow his passion, which should encourage other people in the later stages of their careers to consider making a pivot. I like Scott's story because I regularly meet with people who want to make a move but who hesitate due to their fears and doubts about the viability of the move working out. Nothing is wrong with being afraid of a significant career change. It's natural and understandable. Not only is change hard, but significant career changes come with fears about maintaining satisfactory levels of income and benefits. Here is an excerpt of my conversation with Scott about how he confronted his fears and worked through them:

ME: Were you afraid when you went into nonprofit full time that you were not going to be able to go back to for-profit work? That you were burning a bridge, so to speak?

SCOTT: I was a little apprehensive for quite some time about switching gears from for-profit to nonprofit. However, I finally decided to do something I truly believed in and was passionate about. I came to the realization that it did not matter whether you worked nonprofit or for-profit. If you truly were committed to the mission, the idea, the product, you would become successful . . . I never felt I would be less marketable by moving to nonprofit because I was still selling, still contributing to the bottom line of the organization.

Scott's comments here are powerful. While he was moving to a new industry (nonprofit), he still brought with him core abilities and talents that he could equally apply in this new arena. In other words, he was not starting from ground zero, and he saw this less as a career change and more as a new domain/industry where he could apply many skills he had spent his professional life building and where he could also learn many new things. And before he made this move, he already knew from his volunteer work/career laboratory that he liked this work a lot.

This is a great perspective that I encourage others to bring as we confront a new world full of more possibilities than were ever visible before. Perhaps making moves to new industries or verticals does not require starting from the beginning, and maybe there are more places where you can apply your talents than you realized. And just as importantly, within our hobbies and volunteer work, we can learn new skills and, in some cases, convert them into new career paths. It all begins by being curious, doubling down on your growth mindset, and seeing your career as a continual process of learning. Instead of seeking job promotions, we should be seeking to promote our learning.

3

MANAGING YOUR CAREER IN A DYNAMIC WAY

GET A LIFE: THE POWER OF WHAT YOU DO AFTER WORK

Jeanne Feldkamp was working a regular marketing job in San Francisco when an idea struck her. Her husband, Dan, a software designer, had traveled to Paris and spoke of an "underground supper club," in which ordinary people launched pop up restaurants in the city.

So the couple started Hearsay Supper Club in San Francisco. For a fee, she and Dan entertained strangers at their Dogpatch home with wine and homemade meals. Eventually, Hearsay Supper Club caught the notice of Airbnb CEO and founder Brian Cheskey, who attended one of their meals.

"It definitely wasn't a career move," Feldkamp said. "It was a project that we took on because we thought it would be a fun experiment and a way to meet people and cook for them and give them something hopefully enjoyable in just a different way than we'd seen before."

Feldkamp has always been curious. But what sets her apart from most people is that she acts upon that curiosity. What initially begins as a hobby or personal interest tends to blossom into a string of rewarding opportunities and valuable experiences that keep her relevant in a fickle job market.

"It was a different way of applying a lot of what I already knew about marketing for sure," she said. "Bringing people into our home. And this one-on-one customer service is not something you usually do with software products."

The couple eventually quit their day jobs and moved to Oregon, where they are planning to open their very own wine bar.

We tend to divide our lives into categories: work and nonwork time. We work Monday to Friday from nine to six and then relax on nights and weekends. During our free hours, we might just hang out with friends and family or pursue a hobby or sport.*

But as the job market becomes increasingly unpredictable, the distinction between our professional and personal lives becomes more blurred. Since we can no longer count on career stability, we must adopt a more careful and deliberate approach to how we spend our time both inside and outside of the office.

> *Since we can no longer count on career stability, we must adopt a more careful and deliberate approach to how we spend our time both inside and outside of the office.*

---

* Clearly, COVID-19 has completely changed the game for now, and as of today, it's unclear how long this merger of home and work will continue. The whole world suddenly woke up to a reality in which the family home had turned into an office and a school.

Increasingly, how we spend our off hours can impact our broader careers in both obvious and nonobvious ways. We got a glimpse of this in chapter 2 from Scott Lohmann and Arielle Lapiano. What might initially start as a hobby, passion project, or simple social event could lead to valuable connections, additional skills, industry intelligence, or even a new business or job opportunity.

"The thing is, we already have these skills, and we use them all the time, probably subconsciously, every day, one way or the other," Jenny Darmody, careers editor for the Silicon Republic, wrote.[*] "We are just not used to calling them out and mindfully saying, 'These are important. I need to work on them when day-to-day opportunities arise.'"

Take the Feldkamps—at first glance, a supper club has nothing to do with software. But the couple forged a new career path using the entrepreneurial, marketing, and culinary skills they had acquired from both their day jobs and supper venture. What began as a fun side activity morphed into a new business.

LOOKING FOR A JOB WHEN YOU DON'T HAVE ONE IS TOO LATE

We have a habit of only looking for a job when we need one. But the best time to explore future career possibilities is when you already have a job. Building the habit of keeping your eye on your next move is a vital career strategy today. We should always have our eyes open to what is possible today relative to our work and careers.

---

[*] https://www.siliconrepublic.com/advice/future-of-work-individual-employees.

> *Building the habit of keeping your eye on your next move is a vital career strategy today.*

"This is really an important insight for people to understand," said Sally Thornton, CEO of Forshay. "Too often, people only put their heads up when they make a job change. Otherwise, they keep their heads down at their job and work away. It drives me nuts. It's well-intentioned, like 'I'm focused and dedicated,' but it's not the full picture of how great work happens, and it's not in the best interest of their career.

"The best interest of their career is to look up, to think expansively, to have coffee with people regularly or tea or whatever you love," Thornton said. "Then whenever your career shifts, it's not as jarring because you've always been active in your network, and we've always been creating relationships outside of our business." While I don't intend to add more stress to a world of work that seems more uncertain than ever before, if you think you are in a position or company that is immune to change, you are wrong. The question is not if your working world will change; rather, the question is when. We all need to be honest about this fact. This is the world we live in now, and it's a world we created. Today it's imperative always to be looking, growing, and exploring possibilities.

> *The question is not if your working world will change, the question is when.*

For us to build a fulfilling future of work for ourselves, we have to prove that we are more agile than the next person. We need to know we can learn, adapt, and apply new ways of doing things—better than others can. Most importantly, we must keep learning and find joy in the process of discovery. I think we already do a lot of this, but we probably need to be more intentional and conscious about it.

YAIZA'S STORY: LIFE CHALLENGE PRESENTS A CAREER OPPORTUNITY

Eva Rodriguez Labella lives with her husband Juan Luis Vicente in Madrid, Spain. Eva worked for many years to build a successful career in the fashion industry, where she worked her way up inside the L'Oréal corporation, while her husband made his career as a local fireman. In their midthirties Eva and Juan Luis welcomed their first child, named Yaiza, who was born on Christmas Eve in 2009. Not long after Yaiza was born, her parents noticed that her habits around the home and her interaction with others were different from other children's. She was extremely quiet; she did not speak at all, and she did not play as other children would play. The more they went to see doctors and specialists, the more they became aware that what Yaiza was experiencing was highly uncommon and not easy to diagnose.

Finally, when Yaiza was sixteen months old and after the family had seen many child experts, they were able to diagnose her condition as Dup15q syndrome, which is extremely rare.[*] Features that may be present in a person with chromosome 15q

---

[*] According to the National Institutes of Health, Dup15q syndrome is "a chromosome abnormality that occurs when an extra (duplicate) copy of the genetic material located in the long arm of chromosome 15 is present in each cell . . . The signs and symptoms of chromosome 15q duplication vary significantly from person to person, depending upon the size and location of the duplication and which genes are involved."

duplication include developmental delay and communication difficulties, among other things.

Even before this diagnosis, Eva and Juan Luis experimented with a whole host of ways to try to engage their daughter and to communicate with her. When Yaiza turned three, Eva and Juan Luis were told to take her to the Institute for the Achievement of Human Potential,* founded by Glenn Domann, located in Philadelphia, Pennsylvania. As Eva recalls, "This is where we got trained to perform a stimulation-intensive program that we would have to do with Yaiza six to eight hours a day, every day for three years! They called it VIP—a very intensive program."

As you can imagine, this level of exceptional attention for their child was a huge undertaking, especially for a couple who both held full-time jobs. As they worked through three years together, they both held onto those jobs, in part helped by the flexibility of Juan Luis's schedule as a fireman and Eva's ability to work at home from time to time. They were committed to making it work. VIP required working on so many things with Yaiza to stimulate her brain and neurogenesis. They had to work through a physical program, a sensory program, a special diet, a respiratory program, and an intellectual and social program.

As Eva tells it:

"We had to essentially transform our house and build many things for her to work on balance and strength. It was crazy. Our house was like a gymnasium, with mats all over the place. She had to crawl, for example, like eight hundred meters every day at first. Once her movement got better, she had to run a mile every day and then do patterning on a massage table. We did this

---

*   https://www.iahp.org/about-us.

every day for eight hours, seven days a week, 365 days a year. In the beginning she took to it like a game, but you know, she's just a child, and after a month she started to get bored with the routine. This was when we discovered something that would change our lives even more—we discovered that Yaiza really responded when we told her stories, so I told her thousands of stories while we were doing our programs and exercises, and she loved it. I would even tell her stories while we were running our mile together."

After years of effort, Yaiza started to communicate and connect with the world. As Eva recalls, "Around the age of four, she went from not talking at all to being fluent in English and Spanish. It happened almost overnight, and it was not like she started with baby talk; she went from zero to ten literally overnight, no talking to fully formed sentences and thoughts in both English and Spanish! We were blown away. We knew she could understand us before she started to speak because if we asked her to close the door, for example, she would always do it."

VIP worked. By the time Yaiza was six, she was ready to attend primary school at a "regular school" with some special assistance. "We decided then to focus more on the attention and intellectual part of her development. It was then, after years of experimentation and learning and trying hundreds of different things that we had learned, [we realized] Yaiza learned better through watching specific YouTube videos than she did within a classroom. I was forty-one at the time, and my husband was thirty -nine, and this began our YouTube adventure." The discovery of YouTube as an ideal platform to inspire and teach Yaiza came from a recommendation from a therapist who suggested that Yaiza watch a specific YouTube video to learn the rules of how to play a particular game. They immediately observed that Yaiza learned very fast by watching YouTube videos that explained how to do things and that they had a dramatically positive effect.

Given that they already knew that Yaiza loved stories, and given that there seemed to be a shortage of good YouTube videos that showed kids how to do things, Eva and her husband decided to make the videos themselves. Had they ever made a YouTube video before this? No. Did that scare them away or make them hesitate? No, not at all. Since this was a path that could build a better life for their daughter, it did not take much time to arrive at this decision.

> *I did not wake up at the age of forty and say, "Hey, I want to be a YouTuber!" It just happened.*
>
> —Eva Rodriguez Labella

"I did not wake up at the age of forty and say, 'Hey, I want to be a YouTuber.' It just happened." Eva recalls that it was in November of 2015 that she and Juan Luis decided to create content on You-Tube. "In January 2016 we launched our first YouTube channel,* which was called 'The Strawberry Fairy,' who was me in disguise. You could never see my face, just my hands, and I had a magic wand, and the story was of a fairy who was born without wings, and she had to work very hard to find her real talent. She discovered that her talent was creating the best magic in the world, and this magic was created by telling stories!"

In the beginning, they uploaded four videos a week, all only ten minutes long. "So we were going along for a while, and we

---

* https://www.youtube.com/channel/UCOIngTJRqH2M2KgGyAKi6Yg.

had about one hundred subscribers, and our top video had one thousand views, which at the time we thought was amazing. Well, a few months into it, we were on a flight to NYC, and I remember as the plane landed and I turned my phone on, something crazy happened. In eight hours one of our videos had generated a million views—all while we were in the air. We don't know why or what happened, but one of our videos went completely viral! It was not our best video, but it was four months in, and *pop*, there we went."

After about a year of doing this, a toy company approached Eva to join them full time. They had seen her work on YouTube, and, ultimately, they hired her away from L'Oréal while she continued to grow the YouTube channel with her husband.

A year ago, at the age of forty-four, and in response to the urging of her kids, Eva quit her corporate job/life to focus 100 percent on building out the family YouTube enterprise.

There are so many fascinating elements of this story. Eva's career path and the story of how she got to be a YouTuber is so revealing about what is possible today. She had a great, long career with L'Oréal. Yet despite her age, she adapted to become a highly successful YouTuber, and she built an enterprise with her husband that grows today. As Eva says, in thinking about her life today and her career, "I love the diversity. I feel completely alive. Yes, it's challenging learning new things, but I am extremely engaged and loving what I do and how it allows me to be close to my family. There is still so much I want to do and to learn." Eva never had a grand plan. Before building the YouTube business for her daughter, Eva thought she would retire with L'Oréal and work there for the rest of her life. But her curiosity and growth mindset opened her eyes to new career possibilities.

> *I love the diversity. I feel completely alive. Yes, it's challenging learning new things, but I am extremely engaged and loving what I do and how it allows me to be close to my family.*
>
> —Eva Rodriguez Labella

As of the publication of this book, Yaiza is ten years old and to this day does not know her mother is the Strawberry Fairy. Labella and her husband recently published a book, *Hada De Fresa** (*The Strawberry Fairy*), and they just launched a podcast series as well.[†] Stepping back, we can learn a great deal from Eva and her family:

- The power of experimentation
- The pivot to a new career unexpectedly as a result of life circumstances
- The pivot to a new career path even when you are at the top of your current career
- Joining forces with your spouse, tinkering and experimenting "after hours," and finding great joy and fulfillment from something that just a few years prior you did not even know existed.

This is the future of work. It is happening now.

Feldkamp and the Labella family show us that there is fertile ground outside of the usual places we go to think about work and careers. We are surrounded by opportunities to discover

---

*   https://www.planetadelibros.com/libro-hada-de-fresa-el-hada-que-nacio-sin-alas/310236.

†   https://podtail.com/en/podcast/hada-de-fresa/.

new paths—in our hobbies, in community volunteer work, and in our own life experiences outside of work. The question is, are your eyes open to these opportunities?

BUILDING AN INDISPENSABLE NETWORK

We cannot know everything in a world that continues to change at a frantic pace. But there is something far more valuable than knowing stuff: knowing people who know stuff.

"I think that people get trapped into thinking that skills will keep them safe," Jeanne Feldkamp said. "If they just know the right thing or study the right thing, they'll always be employable. But I don't think that's it. It's always about the strength of your network. The stronger your actual human relationships are, the easier it's going to be to navigate whatever happens with the economy."

> *It's always about the strength of your network. The stronger your actual human relationships are, the easier it's going to be to navigate whatever happens with the economy.*
> —Jeanne Feldkamp, co-founder, Corollary Wines

"With the exception of one single job, every job I've gotten has been through a friend of a friend," she said. "People should really invest in making sure that their friendships are strong, their networks are strong, and they're meeting people and always connecting with other people."

I could not agree more. And as you consider making your next career move, be conscious that some companies are much better environments for you to grow your network than others.

Between 2009 and 2012, I had the great honor of working with Reid Hoffman, founder and chairman of LinkedIn. Hoffman was famous for saying that in an era where things are continually changing, who you know is becoming more important than what you know. This was an essential foundation of LinkedIn, and he was spot on.

> *There is something far more valuable than knowing stuff: knowing people who know stuff.*

We have all called a friend to help us with a difficult problem at one point or another. In my career I have lost count of the times I have needed to ask for help from people in my network.

HOW NETWORKING SURPRISINGLY CHANGED MY LIFE

Over the course of my career, I have benefited from my network in surprising ways. I want to share two stories in particular. Back in 2007 I was interviewing a woman named Lewisa Anciano for a leadership role on my HR team at PMC-Sierra, located in Vancouver, British Columbia. I was impressed by Lewisa, but for several reasons, unrelated to Lewisa's qualifications, I did not hire her. Over the years we kept in touch, sharing ideas and articles and helping each other out when we could. I moved out of Canada back to the United States in 2009, and we still kept in touch. In 2019, over ten years later, Lewisa reached out to me and asked if I would consider applying for a board of directors position in a company where she was working. I had told her it was a goal of mine to be on a board many years earlier. Today I sit on the board of that company, Perk Labs, and I marvel at how someone I interviewed but did not hire for a job became a valuable part of my network and led to me achieve a big career goal of mine. And I was finally able to work with Lewisa, which also was a career goal of mine.

The second story involves how I found one of the most important jobs of my career at a kid's birthday party. In 2009, as I mentioned earlier, I was an HR executive at EA, which made me a very cool dad in the neighborhood and allowed me to play video games guilt free. EA had a fantastic campus, complete with an onsite childcare center. All three of my boys went to that center, so I would regularly have lunch with them, which I loved. One day, my son Connor was invited to a birthday party by a classmate. During the party, I met a man who was married to an EA employee but was in the process of negotiating an offer with LinkedIn.

I told him that I was happy to help him try to negotiate a better offer with LinkedIn since I had a great deal of experience negotiating compensation. He took me up on it, and we spoke on the phone a few times afterward. I'm not sure I helped him negotiate a better deal, but I might have helped him understand his offer terms better. Ultimately, he got the job. A few weeks later, he reached out to me and said LinkedIn was hiring its first head of HR and that I would be a great candidate. Initially, I wasn't sure I'd be interested, but he pushed me to consider it, and I finally agreed to an interview. After interviewing at LinkedIn, I couldn't sleep for a week, I was so excited. I had never wanted a job more. After about a week, I got the job offer. To this day I marvel at how a kid's birthday party unlocked my path to a phenomenal opportunity that fundamentally changed the trajectory of my career.

We meet people every day in our lives, at work, in interviews, at birthday parties, at sports events, cafés, and conferences. You never know how a chance encounter might change your life. Networks not only unlock opportunities; they also help us learn and grow. The more diverse our network and the more alive it is, the more we stand to benefit.

THE PERSONAL BOARDROOM IDEA

Zella King and Amanda Scott believe one of the challenges with networking is that people often perceive the idea of networking to be insincere and self-serving. In 2012 King and Scott set out to help people reimagine networking, and they built out an idea called the Personal Boardroom.*

"At the time I was a business professor doing research on how people take control of their careers and the networks that really successful people build up around them," King said. "I was aware of useful ways to think about networks in the academic world. Amanda was working as a career coach, and she had coached a lot of people who didn't seem to have strong networks inside their company. We decided to try and bring together my knowledge of research with Amanda's insight into how people change their behavior to build better networks, something well grounded in evidence that people could easily put into practice."

At first the duo offered specialist coaching on networks, but King said that fell flat. People felt networking distracted them

---

* To learn more about Personal Boardroom, go to: https://www.personalboardroom.com/.

from their day jobs, and they were not prepared to invest in it. Ultimately, King and Scott decided to help clients identify a group of people who could help them develop their careers just like a board of directors would advise a company's CEO on how to run the company.

"To get away from people's hang-ups about networking, we started asking, 'Who is in your personal boardroom?'" King said. "We wanted people to think about who at the heart of their network is really helping them to succeed. Are they investing in the relationships that can really help them keep fresh and up-to-date and to have impact?" The Personal Boardroom model helps people answer this question by showing them the twelve roles their boardroom members need to play, such as navigator, sponsor, and nerve-giver.

© Personal Boardroom. Reproduced with permission.

Reframing networking into the need to have a career personal boardroom is genius, as people immediately understand the value and hence can take action. It moves from the visual of an awkward cocktail reception with strangers into a model designed to turbocharge future prospects.

Your network today offers you significant career insurance. It should not be underestimated, especially as the world continues to be more and more complex. The more people on your team helping you navigate this complexity the better.

| *Your network today offers you significant career insurance.*

As mentioned in the introduction, one of the most noteworthy trends revealed by the Bureau of Labor Statistics* is job tenure—how long people are staying with one organization. In a world where more people are leaving a company faster than ever before, the average size of an employee's network is growing. The more places I work, the more people I know. A workforce that is more fluid than ever is a workforce that has the potential to be more connected than ever before. My intention here is not to encourage you to leave your company to grow your network. I realize that to build a solid relationship with someone in your organization, for them to see the quality of your character, your work, and your learning agility, you will need to be there for a period of time long enough for that to be established.† Still, I

---

* For information about the Bureau of Labor Statistics, see https://www.bls.gov/bls/infohome.htm.

† I am often asked, "How long should I stay in a company?" or "How will it be perceived by future employers if I leave after a year or two?" This is a hard question to answer directly because different hiring managers have different perspectives on the value of staying or leaving within certain time windows. There is no exact timeline that makes it "okay" for you to stay or go. The key factors to consider in contemplating a move are: Am I learning, growing, and developing and becoming more valuable? Am I being fairly rewarded and recognized for my efforts? Is my network growing, and am I meeting and working with people who can help me in my career growth in the future?

want to call out that we are moving toward a more networked workforce than ever before. I think there are significant upsides to changing employers that will help us find the right jobs and the right jobs to find us through our growing networks.

NETWORK STAGNATION VERSUS EXPLOSION

Early in my career, I worked for Fireman's Fund Insurance Company (FFIC) as a human resources representative. Nestled in the countryside of northern Marin County, just above San Francisco, FFIC was a great place to work, so much so that most people stayed there for their entire working lives. This was my second job out of college, and I loved the people and the culture, especially the fact that it was only a seven-and-a-half-hour workday. While I was there, my network grew inside the company but not externally. I had no idea of the value of building an external network at the time. After four great years at FFIC, a recruiter called and asked me to interview for a job in Silicon Valley. I jumped at the opportunity. I ultimately interviewed and was offered an HR manager job at computer chip maker, Advanced Micro Devices (AMD).

If you do leave a company before two years of service, you may have a great reason. For example, I left EA after less than two years because the primary job I was hired to perform (acquisition integration) was frozen due to the 2008 recession, I did not really enjoy the work I was doing, and I had a once in a lifetime opportunity to build the HR function at LinkedIn. In addition, EA was struggling as a company, and one day my boss told me, "Decisions here are governed by drama, not data." I did not fit in that culture. Who could blame me for leaving less than two years into my time with EA? I could explain why I left early to anyone who might have an issue. Was EA happy I left? No, not at all, but the employees understood and wished me well. I had never worked for a company more than six years and never for less than three before I left EA.

It was 1994, a period of massive growth in Silicon Valley. What immediately struck me was how often people moved between companies. Within a year of my arrival, friends I had made at AMD had moved to new jobs at Oracle, Apple, Cisco, Intel, SGI, and Yahoo!, to name a few. I didn't realize it at the time, but my network was exploding. I did not understand how this would benefit me and my career until a colleague who had left AMD to go to Cisco called and told me he had referred me for a job in his company.

Rodney Jackson, a former AMD colleague, reached out to me about a position on Cisco's mergers and acquisitions integration team. Rodney knew I did good work; he knew my personality, and I think he also knew what kind of role would best suit my abilities. We had worked together closely on many projects. I interviewed there and was offered the position by Mimi Gigoux, whom I discussed earlier. At the time (1998) Cisco was a *hot* company,* and their stock was growing, as was their brand. By comparison, Apple was struggling at the time, and hardly anyone thought Apple would become what it is today—one of the most valuable and revered companies on the planet.

The Cisco job turned out to be a game changer for my career on every level. The people I met at Cisco were the most talented people I had been around in my career, and the teamwork and comradery were unlike anything I had experienced. My time at AMD was fantastic, and there were many outstanding people there too. The network I built at AMD and Cisco has been the foundation for virtually every professional opportunity that has come my way since then.

---

* "On March 27, 2000, Cisco became the most valuable company on earth with a stock market capitalization of \$569 billion." https://www.networkworld.com/article/2229885/cisco-s-storied-past-as-the-most-valuable-company-on-earth.html.

> *I was very fortunate early in my career to have stumbled into a place in the world where talent movement was so prolific that I was able to build a network so powerful it would present me with many great opportunities over time.*

I was very fortunate early in my career to have stumbled into a place in the world where talent movement was so prolific that I was able to build a network so powerful it would present me with many great opportunities over time. I had no idea *this* is what people meant when they said, "Your network matters." It does!

One of the reasons Silicon Valley is home to so much innovation is because its networks are bigger compared to other regions of the world. A recent study published by LinkedIn* determined that on a global level, technology firms have higher turnover than any other industry. These two facts are related. Higher turnover builds more extensive networks, and greater network traffic enables the exchange of more intelligence and ideas.

When we look at organizations that are thriving today and companies who weathered having to make significant changes during COVID-19, technology companies are leading the pack.[†] While many people think high turnover in organizations is a bad thing,[‡] I think they are ignoring a powerful macro benefit from a high-turnover environment: richer and better networks and hence a higher flow of ideas, which is the precursor to innovation.

---

*   https://business.linkedin.com/talent-solutions/blog/trends-and-research/2018/the-3-industries-with-the-highest-turnover-rates.

†   https://www.cnbc.com/2020/05/04/big-techs-earnings-prove-its-immune-to-the-coronavirus.html; https://thehill.com/policy/technology/494439-tech-giants-poised-to-weather-coronavirus-storm-better-than-most.

‡   https://mpstaff.com/the-ugly-truth-about-employee-turnover-in-silicon-valley/.

I am not trying to make the case here that every company should aspire to have high turnover, and clearly every organization should always strive to retain great talent. However, the point I do want to land is that perhaps we have overvalued employee retention and undervalued the power of movement and how that can contribute to a highly connected nerve center for employees and their futures.

> *Perhaps we have overvalued employee retention and undervalued the power of movement.*

If you are at a place today where you are considering the pros and cons of a new job in a new organization, I strongly encourage you to assess the network-additive component of the opportunity. If you work in a place with great people who, over time, move on to bigger and better things, there is a good chance bigger and better things will find you too.

> *The notion of career safety has shifted from being stationary to moving.*

Another exciting dimension I see evolving in the world of work is how the notion of career safety has shifted from being stationary to moving. Said another way, career security used to be considered as remaining in one organization for an extended period—a minimum of five years. The notion was, the longer you worked there, the more loyal your employer was to you, and the more immune you were to job loss. Today, I believe the notion of career safety has shifted to a belief that the more you change companies, the more you learn, the bigger your network becomes, and hence, the more likely you are to find work if you do lose your job or are in a company that becomes disrupted by a competitor.

THE ART OF THE HUSTLE

To remain relevant in a changing economy, we must put ideas and creativity into action even when we're "off the clock." And in an increasingly uncertain world, it makes a lot of sense to consider alternative ways to earn money, even if they are not your primary source of income.

Thanks to high-speed internet, mobile devices, and social media, people are creating, promoting, and distributing content across the world: videos on YouTube, blogs on WordPress and Medium, articles on LinkedIn, music on SoundCloud, and pictures on Instagram.

People are increasingly pursuing side hustles to earn additional income. Witness the emergence of the gig/freelance economy in which people drive for Uber or Lyft, deliver groceries for Instacart, host travelers and tourists for Airbnb, or allow others to rent their cars via Turo.

The polling firm Gallup estimates that 35 percent of US workers are participating in the gig economy, and PYMNTS.com estimates that 40 percent of Americans derive the majority of their income from gig work.

This convergence of technology, creation, and hustling creates an ideal environment for people to pursue personal projects rooted in hobbies, social causes, or entrepreneurship.

They can even raise money thanks to online crowdfunding sites like Indigogo and Kickstarter. These projects might lead to other career opportunities, especially in an increasingly unpredictable job market.

Research shows that personal activities can boost your professional life. In 2014 the Copenhagen Business School in Denmark and the Munich School of Management in Germany published a study that examined 4,138 inventions from twenty-one European countries, the United States, and Japan in all major industries. The academics then measured "organizational creativity" by looking at the financial value of the underlying patent and the "degree of radicalness" of the invention.*

The study found that inventors who continued to ponder their work outside of the office and who pursued a wide range of hobbies ultimately produced higher-quality innovations for their employers.

"We find that employees who continue to think about their workplace research while away from work produce more valuable inventions," the study said. "Diversity of hobbies, more socially oriented hobbies, and more focused hobbies are also positively related to invention value."

Researchers identified specific benefits from leisure activities.

"Employee inventors may be able to use skills developed while pursuing a hobby—such as a disciplined approach to problem-solving—to address problems at work," the paper said. "Second, they may have access to external knowledge sources that may not be available during work time, and that may be combined with workplace knowledge to produce valuable inventions.

"Third, employees may benefit indirectly from hobbies,

---

*   https://pdfs.semanticscholar.org/2dff/57380f69d1c2e41212c95a7abef22a561791.pdf.

since leisure-time activities have been shown to play an important role in the development of cognitive skills: an ability to analogize and the capacity to engage in divergent thinking."

Arielle Lapiano, the director of communications at Paul Hastings law firm in New York, said she often felt restless with her day job.

> The number of ways you can supplement your "day job" has exploded in the past ten years.

"One of the things that I feel sometimes I'm missing at my day job is more of a creative outlet," Lapiano said. "I work at a law firm, which is generally a conservative place, so I can't have as much fun as I'd like sometimes."

So she found a second career by exploring her passion for female empowerment. She recently started a company called Shattered Glass Tees, which makes T-shirts, pillows, and handbags adorned with inspiring slogans for girls and women. Lapiano also regularly speaks about her ventures.

"I found sort of another way to evolve the company to sort of meet my professional aspirations and also sort of check those passion boxes for me," Lapiano said.

"I think the company is definitely leading to something else," she said. "I'm sort of amazed at the different ways Shattered Glass has taken me to different opportunities since I launched the company. And I'm enjoying the ride. I am going to keep trying to push myself and push the company, and also push the day job to make sure that everything I'm doing is aligned with my values and helping me to grow professionally. And that's what's been happening."

Lapiano's story is a fabulous example of how the world of work is evolving from a one-dimensional reality (I have a job, and I work in a company) to a multidimensional space where we have several jobs/projects that combined fill many of our needs for such things as creativity, passion, and earning a good income. The ultimate expression of how hobbies can turn into real businesses is Etsy.* This platform allows creators of handmade items and crafts to reach millions of consumers. Since its founding in 2005, Etsy has enabled over 2.5 million sellers in 234 countries to sell over $3.93 billion worth of goods on the platform.† The number of ways you can supplement your day job has exploded in the past ten years, and this trend is only expected to continue. Having so much choice and opportunity is a great thing.

COLLABORATE OR DIE

We live an era of collaboration, where friends or strangers get together to create things jointly. Take Silicon Valley, where software engineers regularly participate in "hackathons,"‡ events in which they work on code the same way musicians jam together. Maybe something will come out of it; perhaps nothing will. These exercises not only grow collaboration, but they grow networks as well, as new people meet and work together.

Off the clock, collaboration is also pretty standard farther south in California.

---

*   https://www.thebalancesmb.com/what-is-etsy-1794392.

†   https://www.statista.com/statistics/409374/etsy-active-sellers/#:~:text=As%20 of%202019%2C%20more%20than,million%20active%20Etsy%20buyers%20 worldwide.

‡   For more information on hackathons, go to: https://en.wikipedia.org/wiki/Hack-athon.

Danice Maxine Cabela is an actress in Los Angeles. A lot of time can pass between gigs, but even when Cabela is not working, she is still working.

Cabela and her friend Rob had long talked about working together on a movie. One night at a party, they came up with an idea for a comedy (though Cabela admits they were a bit intoxicated). Over the course of their collaboration, the film morphed into a short film about Asian Americans and mental illness, a topic long considered taboo in the community.*

The friends raised $12,000 from the crowdfunding site Seed and Spark. They wrote, produced, and directed *Forget Me Not*, which they plan to submit to film festivals.

"If I'm collaborating, I'm being pushed; I'm getting out of my own comfort zone." Cabela said. "I know that collaboration is incredibly important for skill sets—but also really just as humans to know that we're in it together. What are the writers going through? How can I make the writers' jobs easier? What can I avoid to make sure I don't get left on the editing room floor?"

Collaboration also allows Cabela to deepen her knowledge of the business and, most crucially, to swap intelligence about what's happening in Hollywood.

Doing so is crucial, she says, because of the fast-changing nature of the movie industry. Streaming services like Netflix and Amazon and content platforms like YouTube are upending traditional studios, so Cabela needs to stay on top of things.

---

* https://www.gallup.com/workplace/240929/workplace-leaders-learn-real-gig-economy.aspx and https://www.forbes.com/sites/elainepofeldt/2017/10/17/are-we-ready-for-a-workforce-that-is-50-freelance/#4943f6243f82.

> *If I'm collaborating, I'm being pushed; I'm getting out of my own comfort zone. I know that collaboration is incredibly important for skill sets.*
>
> —Danise Maxine Cabela

"For our industry, we can't do our jobs for long," Cabela said. "We need to collaborate because in our industry and basically every industry these days, you have to have the ability to connect with other people on layers that are outside of your job description. It feels important because I feel like every industry is changing, so to have connections and understandings of how other people are shifting along with you helps you to understand your landscape more."

Said another way, your network is career insurance.

"Industries are colliding now," said Cabela. "I'm starting to see more crossovers between music and fashion and tech. We can't limit ourselves into thinking that people in your industry are the only people you are going to be working with. The world is constantly changing, so we just have to put ourselves out there."

TAKING CAREER CONTROL

The intent of part I has been to equip you with an understanding of the new landscape of work so you can take control of your future and push away your fears. I don't think any of my suggestions are overly complicated. However, they do require you to look at work and careers differently than many of us have been taught while also unlearning some outdated models of what a successful career looks like.

What feels tricky about building a new career model today is that it requires us to unlearn things that have been firmly imprinted in our brains about what a successful career looks like. This model has been reinforced by parents, relatives, schools, and companies, so it feels hard to shake. And that may be true. Unlearning what was so strongly placed in our minds is hard, but it's necessary.

Many of us were taught that to succeed, you must become great at something—become an expert in your field. Yet today, if you become deeply experienced at one thing or in one industry, you run the risk of finding yourself with fewer career options. Ask anyone who has worked in the banking sector exclusively for a significant period of the past thirty years how they feel about their career prospects today. I have worked with some major banks around the world who are terrified of the competition because companies like Apple, Google, PayPal, and Amazon are taking aim at their market. Banking has been moving quickly from a physical branch to a mobile phone, and banks have frozen like a deer in headlights. Banks don't know technology as well as technology companies do. Therefore, their ownership of the banking world has been in a steady decline. Many who have built careers in traditional banks have been forced to rethink their career choice.

Building a vital career today requires learning agility. This is your career currency for the future, your differentiator. Bhaskar Ghosh, a dear friend who holds a computer science PhD from Yale and who is now a venture capitalist after a distinguished career in Silicon Valley, once said to me, "Employees often focus more on *lifelong earning* instead of *lifelong learning*." If you focus on the learning, the earning will come. Today you must grow your capacity to learn new things quickly and unlearn old models just as fast. Going forward, résumés, CVs, and LinkedIn profiles will be more geared toward demonstrating your learning agility than just where you went to school, where you worked, and what you did. They will focus instead on your learning agility: What did you learn and how fast did you successfully apply it? Employers are going to increasingly desire people who can change, adapt, and grow because that is the reality of business today.

> *Employees often focus more on* lifelong earning *instead of* lifelong learning.
>
> —Bhaskar Ghosh, venture capitalist

Building networks, collaborating, experimenting, and looking for opportunities in your passion projects and your hobbies are the main ingredients for you to thrive in this new world of work. Learning agility is the superpower that will help you weather all the change and uncertainty that lie before all of us.

Be open to new possibilities as you live in this new world of work, and always be thinking about your next move. Always. It is not sneaky or disloyal to be in a company and be thinking about what is next. It's not disloyal to have a side hustle (or two) in addition to your day job. Always looking toward your next move and having side hustles is taking control, being honest, and being realistic, and this is the future of work.

For us to create a better model of work and careers that fits the realities of today, we need to understand the challenges and realities that employers face. So, let's have a similarly honest conversation about employers and how they can rethink their talent strategies, given everything we have discussed so far.

PART TWO

EMPLOYERS

THE CASE FOR NEW TALENT STRATEGIES

As one of my former colleagues, Maryann McLaughlin, said to me a few years ago, "the war for talent is over, and talent won." We have entered an era where employees have more power in the work relationship than at any other point in history.* This is particularly true in knowledge-based, white-collar jobs and acutely so in technical roles such as software development and engineering.

Professionals today have more choices and options beyond working for an established company than at any other point in the recorded history of work.† Beyond the explosion of gig

---

* https://www.washingtonpost.com/business/economy/workers-suddenly-have-more-power-to-demand-higher-pay-and-better-jobs/2019/03/08/6668659c-41bc-11e9-9361-301ffb5bd5e6_story.html and https://www.glassdoor.com/blog/5-reasons-job-seekers-have-more-power-than-they-realize/.

† In fact, some believe one of the biggest career challenges for professionals today is too much choice. https://transparency.kununu.com/10-career-experts-share-todays-common-career-challenges/.

economy opportunities, the world of start-ups is expanding, and more and more people are starting to work in start-ups. In her article "Why Millennials Are Choosing Startups Over Corporations,"* Anna Thorson notes that not only are millennials flocking to start-ups today, but corporations are also trying to portray themselves more like a start-up in the hopes of appealing to more talent.

> *Not only are millennials flocking to start-ups today, but corporations are trying to portray themselves more like start-ups.*

Thorson lists many of the reasons for this trend but mostly cites that the perception among millennials is that a start-up offers greater flexibility, a lack of bureaucracy, and more meaningful work.

Sebastian Muller is a self-described serial entrepreneur based in Madrid, and he helped build one of the best tech incubators[†] in the world, ISDI IMPACT.[‡] Today he mentors, coaches, and collaborates with dozens of entrepreneurs across the globe and in that process has had a front-row seat to see how people think about work and how the notion of what a career means to people is changing. "More and more today, people are seeking

---

[*] https://www.valuer.ai/blog/why-millennials-are-choosing-start-ups-over-corporations.

[†] "A start-up incubator is a collaborative program designed to help new start-ups succeed. Incubators help entrepreneurs solve some of the problems commonly associated with running a start-up by providing workspace, seed funding, mentoring, and training (see list below for a more extensive list of common incubator services). The sole purpose of a start-up incubator is to help entrepreneurs grow their business." For more on incubators, go to: https://www.topmba.com/blog/what-start-up-incubator.

[‡] https://www.impact-accelerator.com/isdi-accelerator-ranked-world-top-5-public-business-accelerator/.

personal growth more than career success. People are wanting to spend time on meaningful experiences and to feel part of something with a big purpose rather than just principally working for a salary or a social mandate." This changing perspective that employees have toward work is supported by a 2017 study conducted by BetterUp Labs, a San Francisco–based leadership development platform.* The study interviewed two thousand professionals and concluded that nine out of ten professionals would sacrifice up to 23 percent of their future earnings for "work that is always meaningful."

Just how profoundly the world of work is changing for companies hit me especially hard one day early in my LinkedIn adventure. Reid Hoffman, the founder of LinkedIn, was being interviewed by a journalist who asked him, "Who is LinkedIn's biggest competitor?" and "Who keeps you up at night?" Without skipping a beat, Reid said something to the effect that he worried more about a company that had not been founded yet than he did about an existing organization, that he was afraid a start-up could come out of nowhere and build a new paradigm that might render LinkedIn obsolete.

That response by Reid struck me. And Reid made this comment when LinkedIn was only about seven years old. After thinking about it for a while, it made complete sense to me, especially when you look around at how many start-ups have taken out entrenched competitors in recent decades: Apple, Spotify, Airbnb, and Netflix, to name a few. If you absorb what Reid said and then think about your company's talent strategy,

---

* https://www.betterup.com/en-us/about-us/news-and-press/workers-value-meaning-at-work-new-research-from-betterup-shows-just-how-much-theyre-willing-to-pay-for-it.

what kind of people, what type of organization, and what type of culture should you build today to compete against a company that does not even exist yet? And how do you do that while ensuring the work you are offering is meaningful?

Another situation that woke me up to the new reality of work was the explosive growth of the scooter industry. In my day job, I help many companies think through talent strategies, and last year I was helping a company navigate a complex hiring challenge. They simply could not hire the talented people they needed at the pace they required. When we looked around, we noticed that one industry that was growing like crazy and seemingly having no problem recruiting was the scooter industry.

In the process, I took a closer look at a company named Bird, which was founded in Santa Monica, California, in September of 2017 and became the fastest company ever to reach unicorn status. It reached a $1 billion valuation in only twelve months!* It was able to hire hundreds of employees in dozens of cities around the world and come out of nowhere to build a business in which its scooters were on the streets of most large cities. Before COVID-19 Bird did not have a recruiting problem. Candidates were running to them.

But through a traditional recruiting lens, Bird should have had a recruiting problem. They could not tell applicants that they had a seasoned leadership team with deep industry experience, because the industry did not exist before 2017. Despite being valued at over one $1 billion, a look at Bird's financial plans quickly revealed that building profit over time would be

---

*   https://qz.com/1305719/electric-scooter-company-bird-is-the-fastest-start-up-ever-to-become-a-unicorn/#:~:text=Founded%20in%20September%202017%2C%20Bird,by%20VC%20research%20firm%20Pitchbook.

very challenging.* Hence, Bird could not promise applicants a stable financial future built on a solid plan of reliable future profits. Last, did any applicant to Bird believe this was a sustainable business and that in ten years people would still be riding scooters? Was this a business that had legs and would last? So, with these facts, why did applicants still flock to Bird?

> *Learning how to build something new makes you valuable in an economy that is always changing.*

As I looked at this, it finally hit me: applicants were flocking to Bird (pun intended) and other scooter-industry competitors because they were drawn by the opportunity to build something new. And in a career reality that seems highly uncertain and unpredictable, developing the ability to grow a new business is highly attractive. This opportunity to learn how to set up a new industry and have a novel learning experience was the draw that led applicants to look past traditional career choice fundamentals. You see, learning how to build something new makes you valuable in an economy that is always changing. If you can grow your capacity to create something new, then you are buying career insurance. Bird and the scooter industry provide us great insight into just how much career choices are shifting. One could make an argument that the real value to candidates at Bird was the opportunity to learn how to grow a new business in a new industry. Applicants were not racing to Bird with an expectation of job security or stability. They sought a rare opportunity to build a new company in a new industry.

---

* https://news.crunchbase.com/news/the-revenue-costs-and-margins-behind-birds-scooters/.

As the world of work continues to evolve, and as employees continue to change their views of work, organizations must consider building new talent strategies that work within this new reality. Employers that still hire based on "Hey, we are a nice place to work, we pay well, we are nice, we have good products, and we have a bright future" need to recognize that everyone says that today. Saying those things does not differentiate you in a universe where employees have more choices than ever before. Companies need to get clearer on why they are a special place to work and how they are different and better than other options candidates have.

Employers must realize there is a new and evolving psychology of employees and how they see work. Therefore, how you recruit and develop them as an organization needs to take this into account. For starters, companies need to think about whether the goal of long-term employee retention or even high employee engagement is worth aspiring toward today. Will having these two goals, for example, be the key to creating value in the new digital economy? Are there other ways, perhaps even better ways, to build value that fit a new reality of work?

> *Long-held assumptions around what attracts and motivates employees need to be reconsidered in light of the new ways employees are thinking about work.*

Long-held assumptions around what attracts and motivates employees need to be reconsidered in light of the new ways employees are thinking about work.

What I aim to do in the next chapters is to help employers start to reinvent their talent strategies in light of this new and evolving way we are all thinking about work. I will reveal to you some impressive people, organizations, and industries that are experimenting with new approaches. In addition, I will show you some organizations that were forced to change and build an entirely different talent strategy. In short, my goal in the next few chapters is to help organizations learn how they can build to win now.

4

NEW TALENT STRATEGIES FOR TODAY

In February 2019 Duke University star power-forward Zion Williamson positioned himself on the left wing of the basketball court. Rolling to his right, Williamson took a pass from a teammate and immediately cut toward the basket.

But as he reached the free throw area, the shoe on his left foot gave out, and Williamson slid to the ground, grabbing his right knee in pain. The entire country gasped.

Williamson was not just the best player on one of the country's best college basketball teams, but professional scouts considered him a once-in-a-generation talent. Though he was only a freshman, people expected an NBA team to take Williamson as the first overall pick in the upcoming draft.

After the game, the basketball world was rife with speculation: Was Williamson going to ever play again for Duke? Or would he just forgo the rest of the season and turn his focus to the NBA draft?

After all, few doubted that Williamson, if the rules were different, would have just entered the NBA draft immediately after high school. But under the NBA's so-called "one and done" rule, players had to wait until they turned nineteen years old before going pro. For the vast majority of aspiring talent, that meant spending just one year in college and then joining the NBA.

In addition to Williamson, two other Duke freshmen were drafted in the top ten that year. So that means that Duke lost three of its five starting players to the NBA after they played just one season.

HOW COLLEGE BASKETBALL CHANGED ITS TALENT STRATEGY

College basketball in the past two decades has experienced a transformation that presents a valuable lesson for employers to draw from today. Twenty years ago, most top-tier basketball players would enroll in college and play at least three or four years before electing to turn pro in the NBA. However, due to some changes in the rules and to the increasingly massive salaries afforded to NBA athletes, many players are electing to leave college after just one year. For coaches in the top basketball schools in the United States, this means every year they have to build a winning team in a matter of months. Coaches used to have years to develop talent, to build teams and groom them for success. Today, the game has shifted to one where you have to create a winning team in a matter of months, and you have to do it *every* year to remain competitive. This is where the expression "one and done" originated.

At Duke, head coach Mike Krzyzewski, known as Coach K, has to build a championship-caliber team every season from scratch. So how does Coach K convince the nation's top players to attend Duke when they have no intention of sticking around? How does he build successful teams year after year, knowing that every year his team will be significantly different?

Such a dilemma is becoming increasingly common in the modern economy. Younger staff are much more mobile, and firms can no longer expect them to stay for more than five years. As was noted earlier, the median length of employment for workers between twenty-five and thirty-five is 2.8 years. The United States and other modern economies are also facing a severe shortage of tech talent, especially among software developers and engineers.

> *"Come to my company so I can help you leave it." I believe this will become the recruiting slogan for many companies in the future.*

On top of this high turnover, the rapid change advanced by new technologies puts employers in a challenging place of being uncertain about what skills they will need to build for the future. This inability to accurately forecast the capabilities an organization will need in the future is unsettling. Companies have to reinvent themselves on the fly, which means, like many employees themselves, they must adapt accordingly to such a dynamic economy.

So how do companies attract talent when they can offer neither long-term stability nor security? How should companies face a reality where people are not staying very long? The answer might sound like a paradox: "Come to my company so I can help you leave it." I believe this will become the recruiting slogan for many companies in the future.

In other words, instead of just offering pay and benefits, companies should consider offering prospective workers *employability*. In an uncertain world, a company will benefit from offering to make their employees *more* employable for the long term—even if they leave the firm. This offer has more value to someone today than the hollow promise of long-term employment within the firm. We need to change the conversation and be more honest about the world of work today. Employers must offer their employees the opportunity to acquire the kind of skills and experiences that will keep them relevant and in demand long after they leave the company. In an era where companies cannot guarantee job security, what they can guarantee is making people more valuable for an uncertain future and helping them even after they leave the organization.

> *In an uncertain world, a company will benefit from offering to make their employees more employable for the long term—even if they leave the firm.*

That could include:

- providing numerous educational and training opportunities, including tuition reimbursement, conferences, and workshops
- allowing them to rotate among several departments and geographic markets so they can acquire a broad range of skills and experiences
- allowing them to start their own businesses and then invest in them
- supporting and encouraging their outside interests and passions, such as charities, hobbies, and volunteer work

All of this sounds counterintuitive. Why invest so much time and money for employees to leave you? Why equip them with more skills if doing so makes it easier for them to leave your firm?

Well, for one thing, you don't really have a choice. Look at the situation Coach K faced at Duke University, where he *knew* his best recruits would leave after just one year. There's nothing he could do about it, so Coach K had to build an entirely new talent strategy. He had to think differently, or he was going to lose. And for those who don't know much about Coach K, he does not play to lose. The promises that Coach K has had to make to his recruits are simple yet profound:

> *Come here, and I will help you leave after one year because I will make you better than anyone else can in just one year.*

Come here, and I will help you leave after one year because I will make you better than anyone else can in just one year.

Come here, learn things you cannot learn elsewhere, and be surrounded by people who will make you better personally and professionally.

Come here because we have a winning culture that will help you the rest of your life.

Come here because even if you do not fulfill your dream in the NBA, our alumni network is better than any other school's.

We will help you land on your feet as a coach, teacher, scout, broadcaster, or mentor.

This last point is critical. Coach K is recruiting based on the notion that your future will be better if you come here. He's telling recruits that Duke will be behind them and help them even if they don't make it in the NBA. Coach K had to adapt and shift his recruiting message from what great things would happen to you at Duke to what great things would happen to you *after* Duke.* He had to accept that people would leave faster than before. Hence his value proposition had to shift toward making that one year amazing and offering support for the rest of their careers. In other words, even without graduating, you were in the Duke family forever, and your career would benefit immensely. That's some promise.

The same principle that Coach K and many other top-tier Division I basketball coaches had to create applies far beyond college basketball. In a world where professionals are leaving faster than ever before, organizations should think about how they can adopt a model similar to college basketball's rather than keep fighting the losing retention battle.

No CEO that I have spoken to in the past two years—and I have talked to hundreds around the world—believes retention will increase in the next five to ten years. They all think it will decrease. Yet still I don't see any of them changing their strategies, and I still see too many holding onto outdated and unconstructive ways of treating departing employees. I still see companies threaten employees who say they may leave or who quit. I'm not sure about you, but I rarely see a company wish you well on your departure.

---

* Making the change in his talent strategy was very hard for Coach K. No big changes are ever easy, especially for a world-class competitor with a proven model that had won many NCAA championships. He held out a long time before he was prepared to accept the "one and done" approach that other top-tier schools were adopting. He preferred his model of grooming teams and individuals over time. A great *Washington Post* article tells of a moment in which, after losing in the early rounds of the NCAA tournament in 2008, he realized "the world had changed . . . we had to adapt." https://www.washingtonpost.com/news/sports/wp/2019/03/14/feature/coach-k-duke-basketball-aim-for-another-ncaa-tournament-title-in-one-and-done-era/.

Over the course of my career, a few companies I left made it clear they were upset I was departing. Some of them questioned my decision to leave. One former boss even told me directly she was confident I would never be a successful top HR executive. I call that the Tony Soprano school of HR: "If you quit, then you are dead to me."* Sadly, some companies and leaders still operate with this ridiculous mindset, completely ignoring the value of a long relationship or the fact that someone might want to come back in the future. And they ignore that all employees can post their sentiments both good and bad on countless sites like Glassdoor.

> *Unlike in college basketball, where if you go pro you can never return to play in college, in the corporate world, people who leave your firm can always return.*

Unlike in college basketball, where if you go pro you can never return to play in college, in the corporate world, people who leave your firm can always return. In fact, "boomerang employees" are becoming increasingly common. A 2015 report by The Workforce Institute at Kronos Incorporated and Workplace-Trends.com found that nearly two-thirds of managers surveyed said they were more willing to hire back former colleagues.

Duke certainly made an impression on Zion Williamson. After hurting his knee, he eventually returned to Duke that year, despite the risk of further injury.

---

* The boss who told me I would never succeed reached out to me years later when I was at the helm of the LinkedIn HR function, sitting in what I humbly considered the best HR job in the world at the time. She asked me if I would consider having her daughter be an intern under me because she wanted her daughter to be mentored by a "real HR luminary." To say I got a kick out of that email is an understatement. Unfortunately, her daughter did not intern at LinkedIn.

Why did Williamson do it?

"I mean this 100 percent when I say it," Williamson said. "If I could come back for a second year and play, I would. Being at Duke was a dream come true for me. It was the best year of my life."*

TAKING THE LONG VIEW

Taking the long view today and understanding where your talent wants to go is a great strategy, especially at the beginning of an employment relationship. Mike Gamson was a colleague of mine at LinkedIn, and today he is the CEO of Relativity, based in Chicago. During our time at LinkedIn, Gamson built and led a world-class global sales organization. He is someone who always lights up a room with his spirit, his humor, and his intense interest in whoever is in the room. Gamson was known to do something when he was interviewing that would often surprise applicants. Many times, the first question he would ask a candidate was "So, let's talk about when you leave LinkedIn. What do you want to be doing, and where do you want to be?" This led some to think, *Wait ... I haven't even started, and we are talking about me leaving?*

Gamson explains:

"I've always believed that the majority of the relationships I invest in will be a part of my life forever. Many of my closest friends are people I met as early as grade school. With that as a foundational thought and the recognition that working for a particular company tends only to average a few years, it's always made sense to me to embrace the truth that our current working

---

*   https://balldurham.com/2019/05/14/duke-basketball-zion-williamson-says-re-turn-duke/.

relationship is ephemeral. Once you acknowledge that likelihood and you really care about the other person's best long-term interests, it makes more sense to help them plan for what comes next for them after this experience. When you care about someone deeply, I think you care about their whole career—not just the part of it that overlaps with me."

> *When you care about someone deeply, I think you care about their whole career—not just the part of it that overlaps with me.*
> —Mike Gamson, CEO, Relativity

Anyone who has worked with Gamson will attest to the fact that he lives this belief. This reframing of the work relationship into something bigger that transcends the time you are in the same company is compelling. Being aware of where individuals on his team wanted to go helped Gamson design the flow of work in his organization to optimize assisting others in reaching their destinations. Having his team know that he cared and was working to help them achieve their career aspirations was inspiring. Like Coach K, Mike Gamson plays the long game, asking:

- Who are you?
- Where do you want to go?
- What can I do to help you get to where you want to be, even if that is outside this company?

And this starts from a framework of a relationship that transcends employment and supports the full career, not just the part when you are working for Gamson.

By taking this approach, you are building a foundation in the relationship that is honest and not contingent upon someone having to stay in the company. Moreover, caring about someone and their future and offering to support them for their whole career is more valuable than mainly caring for someone's future only while they are committed to working for your organization.

> *Caring about someone and their future and offering to support them for their whole career is more valuable than mainly caring for someone's future only while they are committed to working for your organization.*

Ditto is a boutique public relations firm with offices in New York City and San Francisco that also takes the long view in their talent strategy. As CEO Trey Ditto says, "When I interview people, we start from the end—we both know you will leave, so let's have an open discussion around where you want to be when that happens so I can help get you wherever that is, and so neither of us is surprised, and we are collaborating on your success."

At the very beginning, Ditto builds a contract that is not based on how long you will promise to be loyal and stay. He knows that's not realistic. Instead, Ditto starts with a bigger goal in mind—"Where do you want to go?"—and if that is not staying at Ditto on a long-term basis, that's fine. The goal is to be honest and to build a partnership that helps the company and the individual. A new and better contract, if you will.

"What [employees] really need is a place with a great boss who is a teacher and a mentor who can build them and help them grow," said Ditto. "People come to work here because they know they will grow and learn more than anyplace else. We tell them we don't pay as much as the fancy firms, but the compensation in learning by coming here is massive. We tell people that their trajectory will be much better over the long haul if they work with us."

What Ditto has done is shift his recruitment approach from "come here for a long time" to "come here, and regardless of how long you stay, your career path will be better, and your longer-term prospects will be brighter." Trey Ditto knows he cannot offer the experiences that other firms do, and he recognizes that over time people change and desire different things. What Ditto *can* control is offering engaging, hands-on work in many dimensions of PR that the more prominent firms simply cannot match, so he uses that to his advantage in how he shapes his talent strategy. And by starting the relationship with an understanding of where his employees want to go, he can ensure he is supplying them with work that is taking them in the right direction.

> *What Ditto has done is shift his recruitment approach from "come here for a long time" to "come here, and regardless of how long you stay, your career path will be better, and your longer-term prospects will be brighter."*

Framing an employer-employee relationship that continues beyond just the period of employment benefits both parties. It's a more in-depth, longer, and more rewarding relationship.* And it's honest from the very start. Saying you are with someone for the duration of their career is way more meaningful *and* realistic.

---

* Too many firms today are still stuck in the old model of "we are in this for the long haul" and expect loyalty, and employees play the game as well: "Oh yeah, I'm loyal and committed and here for the long haul." But really, if you step back, this dance is a charade; both parties know the relationship could change at any time and that the future is too unpredictable for these statements to be meaningful.

Coach K, Mike Gamson, and Trey Ditto take the long view in their talent strategies. This approach seems refreshingly honest and well suited for a more fluid world of work.

In a world where talent movement is increasing, you will have a competitive advantage if you are an attractive place even for people who leave. This expansive thinking, shifting how you see recruiting away from just hunting for talent when someone exits your firm and toward a system that works for you even *when* people leave, provides you with more options and diminishes your recruiting challenges. Embracing the reality that people may leave allows you to build a system that supports making your talent better for tomorrow, and that makes you a more attractive employer.

Organizations should think of their investments in employees as down payments on a long-term relationship that could still produce dividends down the road.

SEVEN TALENT MODELS FOR TODAY

1. Consulting World Talent Strategy: Join Us, Then Please Leave

The consulting industry was built on a model that expects employees to leave after a few years. On an admittedly simplistic level, consulting firms such as McKinsey, Bain, BCG, Deloitte, PwC, EY, and Accenture have for decades created a relationship where both parties understand that you will leave the firm. The deal is simple:

- You join a consulting firm out of college.
- They train you; you rotate on client projects for a few years.

- You land a job at a client that you have enjoyed working with and whose culture suits you best.
- You keep close to the firm through alumni meetups and net-working events.
- No hard feelings when you leave; no managers upset that you have resigned. What is great about this model is that the firm is supportive, helping you find your next opportunity. * The better the job you get after you work at the consulting firm, the happier the consulting firm is, because their brand grows with your success!

> *The better the job you get after you work at the consulting firm, the happier the consulting firm is because their brand grows with your success!*

And the more successful their alumni are at landing good jobs, the more attractive the consulting firms become as an employer. This is a critical concept that many leaders and companies over-look: people thriving after they leave your firm reflects well on your firm. It can even help your recruiting engine if you do it well. I mention this model to demonstrate that beyond top-tier college basketball, there have been long-standing talent models that are built to expect you will not stay a long time, and they seem to work well. When I speak to my many friends who have worked in the consulting industry, they all mention some com-mon characteristics of these firms:

---

* Consulting firms also need turnover in their firms because they make higher mar-gins from clients where their consultants are more junior and the hourly rates are high. If they have too many experienced consultants, the firm arguably makes less profit. So, they have a financial motivation to move people out and encourage some of their long-tenured employees to leave.

- They are always recruiting.
- Management is trained to help you develop and make you more attractive so that you can leave the firm in a great new job.
- They have highly active alumni networks and alumni resources that stay with alumni over the duration of their professional careers.
- Consulting firms take the long view of their talent relationships.

Building a talent model that accounts for people leaving and even supports it can pay big dividends. The consulting industry has proven this for decades. Not all businesses can pivot to this model 100 percent, and many firms may not want this model.*

---

* I fully realize some of you may be concerned that embracing a more fluid workforce means you are potentially exposing your proprietary information or your intellectual property.

"Why would I want to accept that people can leave when it might put my business at risk?" you ask.

Or "Why should I accept that after I train people on how we do things here, they can leave shortly afterward?"

These are fair questions. So, what options do you have? Well, for one, you can try to require them to stay with legal contracts and noncompete clauses and threaten legal action if they leave to work for a competitor. I call that the prisoner strategy.

- Is that the culture you want?
- Will that bring out their best work?
- Will people who leave want to come back or refer their friends or want to partner with your company in the future?
- Will people go the extra mile for you?

The second option is to build a business and culture so tremendously awesome that people want to stay. A place so great and that they respect so much they would not want to disrespect you and steal ideas if they did leave. A place where they want your company to win even when they have left for another job. These are the two main choices you have. But regardless of which you choose, the fact remains that people are still leaving companies faster than ever, so perhaps planning for this and making investments toward this versus how you keep people from leaving is more strategic than you think.

Still, for those of you facing increased turnover with no end in sight, it should be comforting to see other highly functioning models in play.

In his article "Proof That a Lot of Strategy Consultants Leave after Two Years,"* Beecher Tuttle points out that strategy consulting is one of the hottest professions targeted by graduating students today in part *because* there is no expectation of long-term employment.

> *Strategy Consulting has become one of the hottest professions targeted by graduating students today in part* because *there is no expectation of long-term employment.*

Isaac Morehouse supports this notion that a job can be attractive because long-term commitment is not expected. As founder and CEO of two companies (Crash and Praxis), Morehouse helps younger staff find their way to new careers and job opportunities. Through his work coaching hundreds of employees in their late teens and early twenties, Morehouse ran into an unexpected dilemma. His firm worked hard to get his clients interviews and job opportunities. But when the offers come in, many employees hesitated or refused the offer because they were fearful of having to make a long commitment. As Morehouse put it, "I have had to work hard to coach our clients that they are not giving up their rights if they accept a job and that there may be a lot more upside in working in some of these companies than they may realize."

---

* https://news.efinancialcareers.com/us-en/3000218/why-you-should-look-at-consulting-as-a-career-stepping-stone.

2. The Spin In and Spin Out Model

From 1998 to 2004, I worked for Cisco Systems doing mostly mergers and acquisitions. At the time, the company was on an acquisition binge. In my first four years, we bought over fifty companies and hundreds of employees. It was the Wild West of tech expansion, and many companies like Cisco were acquiring tech start-ups, gambling that the tech they were buying would become a new standard: ethernet, optical, wireless, VOIP, and so on. Nobody knew which new standard would win, so everyone had to place bets. At Cisco we placed many.

Unfortunately, some of the people we acquired did not want to stay at Cisco and soon quit. We completed so many acquisitions that sometimes we would reacquire an individual in two or even three different deals.

Cisco recognized that value creation happens in different forms for different individuals and teams. Hence, it decided to experiment with a different model. Cisco realized it might not be the perfect company for everyone and that sometimes the open market and start-up environment are better settings for innovation and creativity. If high-performing talent did not want to stay, sometimes Cisco helped them start a company outside of Cisco. This was a process we called a "spin out." If the technology worked well, Cisco acquired the business or licensed the intellectual property, and this was called a "spin in." This method was a creative solution to common problems. Some people simply don't want to work for large companies. And some people prefer to work in the early stages of a company or simply in a smaller organization. Cisco's approach also served to keep these employees in the extended family and harness their value differently. It enabled great employees who did not want to work for a big company or for Cisco to remain, creating value in the ecosystem as opposed to joining a competitor or becoming a competitor.

3. The Inside Gig Model

It turns out that gig work is not exclusively for people outside of a large employer. Edie Goldberg and Kelley Steven-Waiss recently published a book titled *The Inside Gig*,* in which they show how organizations can build a new talent strategy where gig work happens within the firm. "In today's competitive landscape, companies need to develop fresh approaches to managing talent by leveraging new technologies and responding to changing business models that redefine employment relationships. It is no longer enough to have the most appealing employer brand, or the best university relations programs, or even a best-in-class workspace because it has become less clear how we define the workforce."[†]

What Goldberg and Steven-Waiss point out is that companies should strongly consider building an internal gig network. As they say, "Rather than acquire new skills by hiring from the outside, the new and quite disruptive reality is that competitive advantage is now based on the ability to rapidly develop and better leverage the talent supply *within* your company." And this is particularly true for large enterprises with lots of diverse talent and experience.

Gig work inside an organization has been around for a while.[‡] W. L. Gore & Associates and 3M Company have used a

---

*   https://www.amazon.com/Inside-Gig-Boundaries-Unleashes-Organi-zational/dp/1928055605/ref=sr_1_1?dchild=1&keywords=the+inside+-gig&qid=1594838005&sr=8-1.

†   Ibid.

‡   When W. L. Gore & Associates started their strategy, it was likely not called gig work, but the essence of the work was similar. It was project-based work and included a

similar model for decades within their firms, both of which have regularly been recognized as great places to work.* These organizations created an open marketplace for work within the company. Generally speaking, most work is project based, and once a project is completed, employees then bid to work on their next project. Project owners can see the performance data of those who are bidding, and the employees are similarly able to see the performance reviews of the project owners. It's a high-performing marketplace in the sense that employees have a say in choosing the work they perform and for whom it is performed.

How W. L. Gore & Associates designs work, how it designs its organization, and how it drives its talent portfolio contribute to why it is consistently one of the most innovative companies in America. The consistent movement of talent, the building of relationships and networks within the firm, and hence the robust exchange and iteration of ideas among the staff are fertile ground for innovation and creativity.

4. Internal Mobility Model

Reid Hoffman, my old boss at LinkedIn, wrote a book in 2014 in which he advocated that employers and employees refer to their relationship as "tours of duty." Just as with a soldier who serves in the military, the phrase suggests a series of finite missions tied to a larger purpose and organization.

"The tour of duty represents an ethical commitment by employer and employee to a specific mission," Hoffman writes. "Like lifetime employment, the tour of duty allows employers

---

diversity of projects over time.

* https://www.greatplacetowork.com/certified-company/1000289 and https://www.greatplacetowork.com/certified-company/1000307.

and employees to build trust and mutual investment; like free agency, it preserves the flexibility that both employers and employees need to adapt to a rapidly changing world."*

Just as a soldier might serve for a certain period in Iraq or Afghanistan, a company "tour of duty" might have employees rotate between different departments like sales, marketing, and operations or between geographic markets. Companies like Spotify, Facebook, Google, and LinkedIn all offer rotational programs.

> *You may have the same title, but you don't have the same job for more than two years, and the more honest we are about that, the better it is.*
>
> —Daniel Ek, CEO, Spotify

"You have a number of years when you perform a job, and then your tour is over, and it's time for you to think about what the next step is," Spotify CEO Daniel Ek said. "I describe them as missions. You may have the same title, but you don't have the same job for more than two years, and the more honest we are about that, the better it is."†

While job rotations are not new, they help enable the company and employees to share knowledge more effectively. Job rotations also eliminate single points of failure because more people know how to perform more roles. In a way, job rotations are the ultimate insurance policy for a high-turnover employee

---

* Reid Hoffman, Ben Casnocha, and Chris Yeh, *The Alliance* (Boston: Harvard Business Review Press, 2014), 251.

† https://www.fastcompany.com/90213545/exclusive-spotify-ceo-daniel-ek-on-apple-facebook-netflix-and-the-future-of-music.

demographic. The more people who know how to do multiple roles, the less vulnerable your business is if someone leaves. Spotify is one of the few companies that has institutionalized movement within two years. They recognize tremendous long-term value from the learning, relationship equity, and exposure to the whole company that active internal movement facilitates.

Altera is another organization that uses internal mobility to their advantage. Kevin Lyman was the top HR executive there from 2008 to 2016, and as he puts it, "At Altera, we managed our employee growth process by encouraging the movement of people into new areas, roles, and functions. We actively intervened to create 'talent velocity.' What this change and renewal process got us in return were employees who wanted to be there for the journey because we provided challenge and change. And we also benefited from voluntary turnover that never ran above 6 percent, and top-performer turnover at less than 2 percent."

Altera and Spotify demonstrate that if you can build the new experiences that provide development for your staff, you are likely to have people stay "for the journey."

Building a model for work inside your company that fosters learning new skills, building internal networks, and providing new experiences is not overly complicated. This is more about investing time to build a model that supports the new psychology of professionals today. It's about having the will and desire to make it happen.

Helping make internal mobility more achievable is the focus of New York City–based PhD Talent Accelerator, founded by the former head of HR of the New York Stock Exchange (NYSE), Philippe Duranton.

Duranton's company has created a real-time AI platform in

which every employee can see the necessary skills and requirements of all jobs in the organization. With this information, employees can see how well their skill set matches up. In other words, PhD allows every employee to see how qualified they are for every job in the firm and what skills they need to build if they want a different job. You may be asking yourself, "How has this not been built before?" or "Why doesn't this exist in every company?" Surprisingly, nobody has ever successfully implemented such a model. What employee would not want the ability to see how they match to every job in a company?

Duranton's approach creates full transparency to opportunities within larger firms that has rarely been possible. Over my career, I have seen dozens of employees quit because they were unaware they were qualified for other positions in the firm. I have also seen employers lose talent because the firm was incapable of recognizing or merely ignorant of the fact that the departing individual could perform other roles. Duranton's solution solves a massive inefficiency with respect to internal career movement.

PhD Talent Accelerator helps organizations keep people longer by showing them more roles and possibilities to explore inside a firm. If employees see they can grow and learn more, they will be more inclined to stay. Plus, it helps staff see where they want to develop and grow based on the jobs they want to go after next. By making more opportunities visible inside your company, you have a higher chance of keeping them.

More and more companies are awakening to the realization that they don't have a good grasp of the skills and abilities of their organization. I know that may surprise some of you, but trust me, having worked in many large firms, I have yet to see a firm with a comprehensive awareness of the abilities of their workforce.* I am not trying to point fingers or lay blame on anyone, but this should not be the case. If you agree that talent is the number one driver of value creation in any organization, and if you believe that talent is the only resource that will innovate and create, then shouldn't you know the abilities of everyone in your firm? Moreover, shouldn't this be about the most critical element you are focused on building internally?

To this day, I remain disappointed to report that the worst-performing systems, and the systems in which most firms invest the least are the people systems. Why do companies still pay more for an accounting system than a system that shows them how to create more value and profit within their team? I find this perplexing. Sadly, for most employers, the focus on being aware of your skills begins and ends during the recruiting process, and this is a massive missed opportunity. †

According to Duranton, "Companies are starting to understand that skill sets are becoming obsolete faster than before, and they don't know what to do except hire more and bring in new people that have the new skills they think they need."

Duranton believes that his solution helps both the employee and the employer be more aware of what is possible inside the company, which is a win-win. "If employees know you are committed and investing in the tools to help them find new ways to grow and learn, they will reward you with more effort and

---

* To be honest, I never achieved this in the organizations where I led the HR function, so it is unfair for me to point fingers or lay blame on others. However, if I were back in those roles today, I would fight hard to achieve awareness of my full talent portfolio.

† To be fair, many good leaders and managers know the talents, skills, and aspirations of the employees who report to them, but in most firms this is where the awareness ends. This information is rarely shared beyond the team or department level, which is a big missed opportunity that needs to be corrected.

retention will increase." If an organization can become more aware of its internal talent, the need for it to hire people with new skills diminishes substantially, resulting in ideally a more productive and higher performing organization.

> *If employees know you are committed and investing in the tools to help them find new ways to grow and learn, they will reward you with more effort and retention will increase.*
> —Philippe Duranton, founder, PhD Talent Accelerator; former CHRO, NYSE

Employers should consider focusing on developing their overall skills inventory instead of just looking at retaining individual employees. Growing the capabilities of your employees increases the number of reasons why employees will want to stay in your firm because they are learning new things and becoming more employable. An individual employee's skill portfolio is a pretty good way to predict how long they will remain at your company. If it's growing, you are likely to see them stay longer; if it's not, then you risk them quitting. Unfortunately, very few organizations are looking at this data. This will have to change.

5. Employees on Loan

Another creative model of employment is for employers to lend out their employees, just as some international professional soccer teams occasionally let other teams borrow one of their players for a specific period.

Khazanah Nasional, the investment arm of the Malaysian government, lets its portfolio companies trade their leaders.

For example, the power company Tenaga Nasional could

send a leader with healthy operating capabilities to work for several years at Malaysia Airlines, acquiring skills in turning around a troubled business, according to an article in the *Harvard Business Review*.

An executive with significant experience in negotiating international energy agreements moved from Petronas, the national oil company, to Telekom Malaysia, where she acquired skills in operating an integrated telecommunications network.

"The employees would get a great development experience, the lending companies would get better returning leaders, and the receiving companies would get top talent, and Malaysia would become an advanced economy by building a deeper pool of leaders."*

6. Building Entrepreneurs—Adobe

Beyond learning through internal movement, some organizations allow employees to flex their entrepreneurial muscles. Perhaps nothing better predicts the likelihood of an employee leaving the company than the person's desire to launch his or her own start-up. These programs, although designed to help employees leave the company, also serve to establish strong relationships between the former employee and the company, especially if the company puts real money behind the employee's business idea. Think about it from this perspective: if you had a business idea and you pitched it to your company's leaders, and they said they were not interested, how would you feel? How differently would you think if you pitched an idea and they got behind you with investment dollars and allowed you to change your job to work on it? Of course you want the latter organization.

---

*   https://hbr.org/2015/01/the-case-for-lending-out-your-star-performers.

Adobe's Kickbox program is one of the more ambitious and innovative programs in Silicon Valley. Any employee can offer ideas to improve any part of the company, no matter his or her department or job responsibility. So a marketer can work on a new software product, or an engineer can focus on ways to improve sales.

Here's how it works: An employee gets an idea, anything from a tweak to an Adobe product to a new area of business for the company. The employee then receives a red box containing reference cards that list six things the employee must accomplish before advancing to the next level. Most importantly, the box comes with a $1,000 prepaid debit card that the employee can spend to validate the idea.

After gathering initial data, the employee then approaches a senior director to "sponsor" the project using money from that executive's budget. After securing a sponsor, the employee receives a blue box, whose contents are unknown. The Kickbox program has produced innovations like a music sync feature and Adobe Lightroom, next-generation software used to edit digital photographs.

7. Hackdays to Innovation Days—LinkedIn

Encouraging exploration, innovation, and creativity can pay enormous dividends. This was a core part of the culture that grew at LinkedIn. Starting in 2007, just a few years into LinkedIn's life, the first Hackday was arranged in such a way as to solve one specific issue. Adam Nash, who drove the creation of the company's first Hackday (and many more after it) recalls:

"It's funny to think about it now, but the original LinkedIn Hackday had an unlikely catalyst. On December 14, 2007, approximately one-hundred-plus LinkedIn employees moved into a brand-new space on the first floor of 2029 Stierlin Court. It was the first time LinkedIn had designed a workspace from the ground-up, and it included a large number of LCD TVs on the wall. The goal was to immerse the product and engineering teams in real-time feedback and data from the LinkedIn community, and small Mac Minis drove each of the TVs."*

The first Hackday was so popular that in time it went from once a year to once a quarter to once a month. In 2010 Hackdays were folded into what is known today as "InDay"—a day a month when any employee can work on a passion project, participate in Hackday, work on a volunteer project in the community, and the like. A fundamental concept of Hackdays, as Nash says, is that "you learn by doing." The Hackday part of InDay later morphed into yet another name: "Innovation Day" (yes, anything special at LinkedIn had to begin with "In"). The way Innovation Day developed is a story worth telling.

In January 2011 LinkedIn acquired a small company called Cardmunch. A few months after the acquisition, one of the co-founders, Bowei Gai, came into my office to pitch an idea. He had participated in several Hackdays and had met Adam and many other fellow hacker evangelists in the company, including Yevgeniy Brikman, Flo Xhabija, Matthew Shoup, and Prachi Gupta. Gai said he had been talking with these folks. They all wanted to enhance Hackdays such that the winners, the best hacks, should be offered the opportunity to pursue their hack full-time and be able to transition from whatever project they were working on at the time to working on the hack.

---

* https://adamnash.blog/2011/05/05/why-linkedin-hackdays-work/. For those interested in learning more about the amazing benefits of Hackdays or how LinkedIn thought about it and applied it, check out Adam's blog.

While we were meeting, our CEO, Jeff Weiner, happened to be walking by, so I invited him in and asked Gai to share his idea. I said, "Jeff, Bowei has an idea that sounds great," and then Gai went over the proposal. Without asking a single question, Weiner said something like, "I love it. Do it." He smiled and left my office—only to come back five seconds later to say, "Wait, before you do that, please check with the VPs of engineering and product to get their buy-in, too, since this will mean their staff may be unexpectedly changing roles." Gai was in shock.

I think he had come to my office ready for a debate and possibly even expecting corporate pushback to his idea. He could not believe that his pitch was made to me and then unexpectedly approved by the CEO in the span of about ten minutes. The VPs of engineering and product also approved the proposal, and it was implemented soon after. Hackdays were and are a fantastic part of the LinkedIn culture. In this case, the way it grew and how it was allowed to flourish driven by employee suggestions are excellent examples of how employers can build trust, belief, creativity, and innovation. How do you think Gai felt about this experience as a new employee at LinkedIn? Do you think it made him want to stay longer and create more? Do you think he shared his glee and amazement on his social network channels and told all his friends? Yes, of course he did.

Allowing your employees to put their fingerprints on your culture can have enormous benefits. I lost track of the number of new products, processes, and ideas that came to life from the Hackdays at LinkedIn, and I credit the leadership and the culture for enabling great ideas like this one to flourish. In this case, a culture unlocked entrepreneurial energy and belief, which in turn unlocked countless new products and improvements regularly in the company.

FROM GOLDEN HANDCUFFS TO EXPONENTIAL UNCERTAINTY

America's entrance into the industrialized age in the late nineteenth century launched the concept of "long-term employment" for individual employees.

The world's vociferous appetite for raw materials and manufactured goods meant companies needed a stable workforce to match supply with demand. So, companies and labor unions negotiated multiyear contracts that set wages, working conditions, and job security.

Eventually, industries like automobile makers in the Midwest lured multiple generations of families with such attractive compensation and benefits that people never needed or wanted to leave—hence the term "golden handcuffs."

But over the past thirty years, the emergence of globalization and the internet transformed the US economy into a more dynamic and less predictable market. Technological advancement has accelerated as more powerful computing chips and internet speeds have allowed companies to do things faster and more cheaply.

"We won't experience a hundred years of progress in the twenty-first century—it will be more like twenty thousand years of progress," futurist Ray Kurzweil wrote in his famed essay, "The Law of Accelerating Returns."*

The rapid pace of technology seemed to upend incumbent industries overnight: retail, newspapers, transportation, logistics, entertainment, communications, and health care, just to name a few. And newer technologies like artificial intelligence, gene editing, autonomous vehicles, 3D printing, nanotechnology, quantum

---

* https://www.kurzweilai.net/the-law-of-accelerating-returns.

computing, and blockchain promise even more disruption.

And just as more innovation begets more innovation, more capital also generates more capital.

Over the past decade, we've witnessed the birth of a new kind of a company: unicorns, private tech firms worth at least $1 billion. Since the great recession, the Federal Reserve has kept interest rates at historic lows. As a result, investors, including mutual funds, university endowments, foreign governments, and pension funds, have been searching for higher returns beyond stocks, bonds, and real estate. Joining them are cash-heavy corporations who are looking for the next big technological breakthrough.

As a result, these investors have focused their capital on fast-growing unicorns like Uber, Pinterest, and Spotify (all of whom have since gone public), allowing them to expand at even faster rates.

From 2001 to 2008, the combined private valuation of all US unicorns jumped more than six times to $600 billion, according to data from Pitchbook. Unicorns three years old or older raised $40 billion last year, compared to less than $5 billion in 2013.

With such financial firepower, tech firms are supercharging their innovation. As a result, companies are already preparing for a future in which their current business models are obsolete. Take Uber—the company has invested billions of dollars in self-driving cars, even though such technology will ultimately replace the freelance drivers that generate their revenue today.

Given such rapid technological change, it's no wonder employees feel less engaged at work and stay fewer years with one employer.

Today, more than 25 percent of the working population goes through career transitions every year. Half of all hourly workers leave new jobs within the first 120 days, according to research conducted for the SHRM Foundation by Talya N. Bauerm, a professor of management at Portland State University.*

> *Companies are already preparing for a future in which their current business models are obsolete.*

"For most of us, departures, whether initiated by the employee or the company, are negative events," author Tamara Erickson writes. "This negativity occurs because conventional 'outs' are shaped by the expectations we convey about the relationship from the beginning—that we want unconditional loyalty and that it will be rewarded (perhaps, 'wink, wink') with a steady career and comfortable retirement. When these expectations are not borne out, due to either party's initiative, bad feelings are the inevitable result."†

> *Branding your recruiting efforts under the slogans of "stay here for a long time" or "grow your career here" may now be worthless investments.*

Branding your recruiting efforts under the slogans of "stay here for a long time" or "grow your career here" may now be worthless investments. Professionals today want financial security, and they also recognize that no industry or job is 100 percent safe from disruption. Thus, they are increasingly seeking organizations that will grow them and keep them prepared for an uncertain future. This should be the promise employers make

---

* https://www.shrm.org/foundation/ourwork/initiatives/resources-from-past-initiatives/Documents/Onboarding%20New%20Employees.pdf.
† https://hbr.org/2013/12/never-say-goodbye-to-a-great-employee.

instead of a promise of job security they know they can't keep.

RETHINKING EMPLOYEE DEPARTURES

I will be the first person to tell you that every company should try to keep their best talent. But I also am here to tell you that you may be underappreciating the value a departing employee can bring to you and your organization. In some cases, they might be of higher value to you than when they were an active employee.

> *Instead of looking at employee exits as a significant setback, we should look at their departure as an opportunity and possibly even a good thing. If nobody ever exits an organization, few new opportunities are created for people to move and grow into.*

Instead of looking at employee exits as a significant setback, employers can look at their departure as an opportunity and possibly even a good thing. If nobody ever exits an organization, few new opportunities are created for people to move and grow into unless the company is growing like crazy. Turnover is a healthy and vital thing in organizations because it creates new opportunities for your staff to be promoted and for you to bring in new talent from the outside.* Plus, if the departure is a positive experience, your exiting star will be more inclined to help you, returning one day or referring other people to you. It's crucial to embrace the many potential positive outcomes from a star leaving over your perception of loss.

---

* As an aside, I can tell you from my thirty-plus years of experience in human resources, several times we have lost someone we all thought was a star or a high performer only to have us hire someone new and discover the new person was far better.

People leaving your firm is not the end of the world. Perhaps the time someone works for you is just the start of a longer-term relationship, as Gamson and Ditto showed us earlier. Maybe the person leaving can continue to provide value to you and your firm long after they depart, and they might perhaps even return one day.

Let me give you an example of what I mean. On May 19, 2011, I had the honor of standing in the bell tower of the New York Stock Exchange with my fellow LinkedIn executives to ring the opening bell and celebrate that we were going public.* As we approached this date, our team knew that our success would increase the value of our employees and lead other companies to try and poach our talent. Going public is quite an achievement, one that many companies aspire to; hence these aspiring companies want people who know how to get that done. We also knew that if our stock climbed, it might make some of our staff see their circumstances differently due to an increase in their financial security. This might lead them to pursue a new path. We were okay with that, but we did not want to be surprised if we lost a key player. We had conversations with all of our top leaders and talent across the organization to ensure they understood their value to us and to assess their plans.

Well, a few weeks before we even made it to the famous

---

* Investopedia explains, "Going public refers to a private company's initial public offering (IPO), thus becoming a publicly traded and owned entity. Businesses usually go public to raise capital in hopes of expanding. Additionally, venture capitalists may use IPOs as an exit strategy (a way of getting out of their investment in a company)." https://www.investopedia.com/ask/answers/what-does-going-public-mean/. Also from Investopedia, "An IPO refers to the process of offering shares of a private corporation to the public in a new stock issuance. Public share issuance allows a company to raise capital from public investors. The transition from a private to a public company can be an important time for private investors to fully realize gains from their investment as it typically includes share premiums for current private investors. Meanwhile, it also allows public investors to participate in the offering"

balcony at the New York Stock Exchange, DJ Patil, who was our chief scientist and chief security officer, tendered his resignation. This was a shock. You see, Patil was an impact player in so many ways beyond just being super in his role. He was a great recruiter and a great spokesperson, he has great charisma, and we knew his loss would be felt across the company. Many people inside and outside of the firm admired Patil. He would be difficult to replace. We met extensively with him to understand his motivations, and when we did, we supported him and asked how we could help. While it hurt to say goodbye, what happened next surprised me.

Even though Patil left the company as an employee, he remained as committed as ever to LinkedIn's success. He continued to refer many great candidates to us. He made himself immediately available any time the team or his former bosses needed him, and he offered his advice and strategic ideas willingly. He kept being a great recruiter for us! As Patil put it to me when we spoke about this many years later:

"The reason I continued to help is that when you build something of importance, you never permanently walk out the door. The mission is just too important. You've put so much energy into it that it becomes part of you. Part of that means making sure great talent can be connected to awesome opportunities within the organization and still providing input to the company/organization on how it can be better. Think about it this way: you've spent all these hours with your colleagues. In many cases, you spend more time with them than your own family. When it's a healthy relationship, you take the long view and continue to help. And that value is returned ten-fold in relationships, future opportunities, and net success."

At the time, I was surprised how much of an impact Patil continued to make even after he left. We were fortunate he remained engaged, and it's a testament to Patil's character and the respect he had for the people and the leadership that contributed to him taking the long view of the relationship.* My experience with Patil taught me that sometimes people who leave your organization can continue to provide substantial benefit.

> *Sometimes people who leave your organization can continue to provide substantial benefit.*

Today, the talent pool, especially the technical talent pool, is pretty thin and likely to stay that way for some time. Companies simply can't afford to write off talent if they decide to leave. Departing staff may return one day armed with even more experience and expertise. They can also serve as strategic advisors and referral engines for more exceptional talent to come your way, as was the case with DJ Patil.

Sometimes your departing employees return. Such "boomerang employees," especially talented women and men who leave the workforce to be the stay-at-home parent or caregiver, offer companies several advantages, author Tamara Jenkins writes.

> *Such "boomerang employees," especially talented women and men who leave the workforce to be the stay-at-home parent or caregiver, offer companies several advantages.*

---

* Unfortunately for Patil, the opportunity he left LinkedIn for did not turn out as he had hoped, but a few years later he was appointed the first-ever chief data scientist of the United States and worked for the White House under President Obama.

"They are familiar with your operations and culture, know many of your current employees and clients, and may require little or no training to start making contributions," she wrote. "Often they are cheaper to hire, particularly if former managers have maintained contact while the employee is away," and they can ramp up quickly.*

Returning employees "will become an increasingly valuable source of talent over the years ahead," Jenkins writes. "In what's perhaps the most frequently discussed example, some women chose to the off-ramp for several years sometime in their career, and many are eager for opportunities to return . . . Regardless of whether their departure is voluntary or involuntary, it's never wise to say goodbye to a good employee." This does not mean you refuse to let them go. Instead, you reframe their exit as an opportunity to receive a different kind of value from them. They can transition from employee to supportive and engaged alumni.

Perhaps the most famous boomerang employee of all time is Steve Jobs.

In 1985 Apple's board of directors, at CEO John Sculley's urging, fired Jobs. Over the next several years, Jobs founded NeXT, which he later sold to Apple. The years away from Apple and his time at NeXT helped Jobs grow into a better leader.

When Jobs returned to Apple in 1997 as CEO, he had matured as a leader, especially as someone who could adapt to changing conditions, Sculley told the *San Francisco Chronicle*.† Jobs still refused to compromise on some things, but he demonstrated pragmatic flexibility that had been utterly absent during his battles with Sculley.

---

* https://hbr.org/2013/12/never-say-goodbye-to-a-great-employee.

† https://www.sfgate.com/business/article/How-John-Sculley-and-Steve-Jobs-hated-and-helped-5812571.php.

Regardless of whether their departure is voluntary or involuntary, it's never wise to say goodbye to a good employee.

—Tamara Jenkins

Take iTunes. Despite loathing Microsoft, Jobs realized he needed to expand the music service's reach to users of Windows, the world's dominant operating system.

"The Steve Jobs that worked with me in 1985 never, ever would have created a product like iTunes and put it on Microsoft," Sculley said. "When he came out with the iPod and iTunes, it was brilliant. It was exactly the right product. It reinvented the music industry, but he put it *on Windows*."[*]

THE POWER OF ALUMNI

Employers need to craft a specific strategy for boomerang employees. They must first make sure that the employee's exit from the company goes smoothly, without any tension or anger. Employers also need to invest in technology and programs that allow them to identify and track talented former employees who might be willing to rejoin the company down the road. Other than some universities, I don't know of many organizations that purposefully track their alumni. Nurturing your alumni community is a great talent strategy for today:

- Keep them close. Send them regular updates on the organization.
- Invite them in to attend or deliver seminars.

---

[*]   Ibid.

- Hold alumni networking events: coffee hours, lunches, or dinners.
- Ask them to come in and be judges for Hackdays.
- Appoint them to advisory boards inside your firm.
- Call them for advice or guidance from time to time.
- Build an alumni mentor program so they can help your employees as well as other alumni.

This strategy requires minimal effort or expense compared to the potential rewards.

"Not every new venture works out," G2 Crowd chief financial officer Ryan Bonnici said. "Some employees leave to try their hand at start-ups, which have a high failure rate. Others work at new companies only to find that the job isn't what they expected, or that the culture isn't the right fit. So these great employees may be looking for work again someday—and you want to be at the top of their list."[*]

For example, energy giant Chevron's Bridges program allows company alumni to land potentially lucrative project work as technical specialists, partner representatives, guest speakers, recruiters, mentors, peer reviewers, and advisors to focus areas.[†]

In a world where more people are leaving companies faster, more companies have larger alumni populations than ever before. This is fertile territory that employers should leverage.

"Establishing a corporate alumni network, which requires relatively little investment, is the next logical step in maintaining a relationship of mutual trust, mutual investment, and mu-

---

[*] https://hbr.org/2018/09/why-i-encourage-my-best-employees-to-consider-outside-job-offers.

[†] https://alumni.chevron.com/chevron-careers/chevron-bridges-contract-positions.

tual benefit in an era where lifetime employment is no longer the norm," Hoffman writes in *The Alliance*.*

> *Alumni groups not only provide employers a pipeline for new (and old) talent but also offer customer referrals and intelligence on competitors and broader market trends.*

Alumni groups not only provide employers a pipeline for new (and old) talent but also offer customer referrals and intelligence on competitors and broader market trends.

"This may be the most counterintuitive point of all," Bonnici of G2 Crowd said. "But when great employees decide to leave on good terms, there can be an upside for the company. Out in the world, they'll be in a powerful position to speak honestly about their experiences. If they leave our company feeling good about us, they'll speak positively about the brand. If they feel good about me, they'll encourage great people to come work for me." We don't just need a new contract between employers and employees; we also need one between employers and alumni.

FROM JOB SECURITY TO CAREER SECURITY

Building a new talent strategy for today starts with rethinking your relationship with your employees. As Gamson, Ditto, and Coach K show us, taking the long view of the relationship is refreshingly honest and a more meaningful commitment than

---

*   Reid Hoffman, Ben Casnocha, and Chris Yeh, *The Alliance* (Boston: Harvard Business Review Press, 2014), 128.

merely a relationship bounded by the time someone works for you. The fears of a disjointed culture, an unfocused workforce, or the inability to deliver consistent results are among the forces that make some employers hesitate to build new models of this relationship. We have been taught that employee retention builds organization muscle, greater trust, and internal coordination, and hence makes us more likely to succeed. However, embracing the fact that we are in a world where talent movement is more frequent can help you build talent strategies that optimize for this new reality. I know for some this is a challenging notion.*

Telling employees you want them to stay over the long term is still a healthy approach. Showing them you want them to thrive over their entire career, beyond just working for you, delivers a stronger message. That's precisely what Chipotle is doing, and it is working.†

---

* For some employers, the rapid employee movement of today may feel unstable and unconstructive, and it's worth pausing to address this concern because it's real. Some ask, "How can you build a culture when everyone is new and some folks who just got here a few years ago are leaving?" Well, the evidence is in. Look around. Companies are being built quickly and realizing profits and high valuations very fast, so we know you don't need long tenure to build successful organizations. Rapid talent movement does not mean no culture is being built; rather, I would argue a very impressive culture of adaptation and complex problem-solving is being built. As I mentioned earlier in the book, during my tenure with LinkedIn over four years, during which we grew from four hundred to about four thousand, our culture was all about growth, on-boarding, building teams, and communication muscle. Creating a high performing culture during hypergrowth is incredibly complex and involves experimentation because you are spinning many plates at the same time—adding staff, new offices, new locations and countries while also trying to be commercially viable and successful. Now this may not be a culture that resonates with you, and it may not be one that fits the framework of your company or your development cycles, but you cannot dismiss the power of a culture that can evolve, change, and adapt quickly. Having a company that creates value while members are regularly joining and leaving faster than before is a potent competitive advantage today, and in some cases if you can build movement and learning experiences from within, you can achieve the reality they have at Altera and Spotify, where people will stay longer.

† https://www.cnbc.com/2019/07/23/chipotle-earnings-q2-2019.html.

By curating your alumni and keeping them close, you are showing your existing employees that you are with them for the long haul. By investing in your alumni, you are proving to your employees that your care extends beyond the time they work for you. You are showing them you are offering something more significant and far more valuable than job security. You are providing them career security.

Taking the long view in your talent strategy means moving from a "retain the employee" strategy to a "retain the relationship" strategy.[*]

---

[*] I want to credit Simon Williams, CEO of NTT Data UK, for introducing me to this expression during a conference in Portugal in 2019.

5

LEARNING VELOCITY

In an economy where specific skills can suddenly become obsolete, it makes sense to hire talent that can move into a diversity of new roles.

Unfortunately, too many companies today still value experience over potential. They focus on what a person has previously accomplished versus what they can achieve. A salesperson is always a salesperson. An engineer is always an engineer. A retail person is always a retail person, a banker can only be a banker, and so on. Experience matters and will always matter. However, I think we need to shift toward a more open mindset on talent. We need to recognize that when we hire someone to do a job today, it's highly probable that within a few months or even weeks, they will need to perform different tasks. Priorities and objectives change fast today. Therefore, shouldn't we put a premium on hiring people we know can adapt as their roles and jobs continue to evolve and change?

In this unpredictable economy, what someone can know

tomorrow and in the future will help us more than what they know today and what they learned in the past.

> *What someone can know tomorrow and in the future will help us more than what they know today and what they learned in the past.*

Your value as an employer will be measured by how quickly your firm can learn and apply new skills—your organization's *learning velocity*. Whatever industry you are in today, you know it will be different next year and the year after. The future will be owned by organizations that can adapt and learn new things faster than the competition. It's that simple. Creating a culture of high learning velocity starts with raising your awareness of all the talent and skills in your organization. Growing your employees is more important than recruiting today. All jobs are changing.

> *Increasingly today and into the future, your value as an employer will be measured by how quickly your firm can learn and apply new skills—your organization's* learning velocity.

Therefore, raising your learning velocity as an organization gives you a competitive advantage. How you build learning velocity in your organization must extend far beyond a classroom setting. The work experience must become the "classroom,"* and jobs need to be created in a way that maximizes the balance between learning and producing.

---

*   For more on this topic, see the article, "Making Learning a Part of Everyday Work." https://hbr.org/2019/02/making-learning-a-part-of-everyday-work.

There is enormous untapped energy when someone tackles something new. We are limiting ourselves if we box people into career frameworks that say if you are a "this," you will always be a "this." Think about your career to date. When have you been most inspired and filled with energy? Was it when you were doing the same thing for an extended period, or was it when you took on something new and different? Something that maybe even made you feel a little uncomfortable?

In chapter 4 we discussed the merits of internal mobility from the perspective of helping people move their careers in a direction they desired. However, there are also enormous benefits to putting someone in a role or a job they had never considered. Many of my previous employers would have never taken such big chances on moving people into very different positions. But some did.

At LinkedIn we regularly asked and encouraged employees to do something different. We took a guy from accounting and had him oversee the company's food operations. We took a financial analyst and had him manage our facilities and build a wellness program. We took a woman from business development and had her lead LinkedIn Japan on an interim basis.

While on the surface these seem like exciting career directions, it's hard to fully capture the outsized impact it had on the employees who made these significant changes. It blew their minds and tapped into a more profound commitment, deeper loyalty to the company, greater trust in leadership, and massive uptick in engagement. People we moved into roles that many would consider "not in their career path" almost always exceeded our expectations. Did every case of putting someone in a new role result in success? No. But most of the time, it did, and when it did, they told the world. This helped grow our brand. The case of the financial analyst at LinkedIn who took on our wellness and facilities administration is worth sharing.

ARMEN'S STORY

In the summer of 2010, as we were nearing the 2012 Summer Olympics, one of our financial analysts asked to meet with me. I soon learned that he intended to offer his resignation. Armen Vartanian was training to be a marathon runner for the Armenian Olympic team. He told me that working at LinkedIn and training for the Olympics were turning out to be incompatible. Armen needed more time to train and sleep, and the long hours and demands of his job as an analyst were compromising his training regimen. He felt he could not fulfill his obligations to LinkedIn, but his dream of being on the Olympic team meant so much to him that he had thought his only choice was to resign. Before meeting with Armen, I met with our CFO, Steve Sordello. We both agreed that the company should try to keep Armen, and at the time this was happening, Steve and I were working to build out a wellness program for our employees.

When Armen came into my office, he was surprised to see both Steve and me in the room. Armen told us his story, handed us his resignation, and hung his head low, and we could tell this was hard for him. That was when Steve and I started to play out our secret plan for Armen—we took the resignation letter from him and right there ripped it up. We said, "No way will you leave LinkedIn!" We told him he was a great person and a pillar of our culture and that we wanted to find a way to support his dreams.

We then told Armen about the wellness program we wanted

to build. We asked if he wanted to develop it for us in a part-time role to allow him to stay with us while also having enough time to pursue his dream. I am not sure how far I got into that before Armen started to tear up, I began to tear up, and even Steve started to get misty-eyed. I will never forget that moment. Armen was moved that we would work with him to help *him* to put *his* needs and dreams first and yet also find a way to have him stay with us and add value in a different role. Did we care that Armen had never built a wellness program before? Not for a second. We trusted he could figure it out, and he did. It's been years since that day in the summer of 2010, but ask any Linke-dIn employee what they think of LinkedIn's wellness program, and you will have your answer. It's world-class.

> *Armen was moved that we would work with him to help* him *to put* his *needs and dreams first and yet also find a way to have him stay with us and add value in a different role.*

After the Olympics Armen took on more work in our facilities organization in addition to his work with wellness, and today he is a senior facilities executive at another firm! That's right. In that one moment when we offered Armen a way to pivot into a new career space, it changed the arc of his life's path in a dramatic way. Today, he continues on that exciting path. This is a testament to our openness at LinkedIn to explore moves like this but also to Armen's courage, adaptability, and his particular learning veloc-ity. We took the long view of Armen and his career.

Armen's story gives merit to the notion that offering new roles and even nontraditional assignments to people can pay enormous dividends. These moves can change people's lives. In the case of Armen, this move also allowed us to keep a cultural ambassador from leaving, which arguably would have hurt more than losing a financial analyst.

IT'S NOT WHAT YOU KNOW; IT'S WHAT YOU CAN KNOW

Learning velocity will command the most significant value in the job market of the future. Instead of looking for people who are experts in a specific area, employers are starting to seek talent that can quickly adapt to whatever role or responsibility employers require of them. Being able to measure a candidate's adaptability and learning velocity will be critical for companies going forward. COVID-19 has only served to amplify this necessity.

Josh Bersin, in a recent *Harvard Business Review* article, reinforces this notion. "The secret to selecting great leaders is to predict the future, not to reward the past," he writes. "Every organization faces the problem of how to identify the people who are most likely to lead your teams through growing complexity, uncertainty, and change. Such individuals may have a very different profile from those who have succeeded in the past, as well as from those who are succeeding in the present."*

Bersin's article was aptly titled "Hire Leaders for What They Can Do, Not What They Have Done." More and more recruiters I work with are looking closely at a candidate's talent and learning velocity. In some cases, they are putting a premium on what you can learn above what you have learned. In other words,

---

* https://hbr.org/2019/08/hire-leaders-for-what-they-can-do-not-what-they-have-done.

recruiters are beginning to measure your prior experiences not just to see what you achieved but to gauge how fast you learn.

USING THE RIGHT LANGUAGE

Throughout the business world today, the growing "skills gap" has dominated the conversation. Companies unequivocally realize that their employees, including future ones, are not prepared for the demands of a digital economy. Our ability to upskill and develop new digital skills is lagging behind the pace of technical change. Therefore, the big question is, what skills should employers develop? Today, that feels like a moving target. How can employers possibly know what skills to develop if technology keeps changing the game and presenting the need for yet another new set of skills to be learned in their workforce? I have worked with many global firms in the midst of implementing a digital transformation. Often the planning comes down to one big question: Are we going to teach our employees the new skills, or are we going to have to hire new skills? The answer may be easier than we think, and the answer may be both.

In the next three years, as many as 120 million employees in the world's twelve largest economies may need to be retrained or reskilled, according to a study by the IBM Institute for Business Value (IBV).* Also, only 41 percent of CEOs surveyed say they have the people, skills, and resources required to execute their strategies.

"Organizations are facing mounting concerns over the widening skills gap and tightened labor markets with the potential

---

* https://newsroom.ibm.com/2019-09-06-IBM-Study-The-Skills-Gap-is-Not-a-Myth-But-Can-Be-Addressed-with-Real-Solutions.

to impact their futures as well as worldwide economies," said Amy Wright, managing partner of talent and transformation at IBM. "Yet while executives recognize the severity of the problem, half of those surveyed admit that they do not have any skills development strategies in place to address their largest gaps."[*]

Companies can start to solve this problem by rethinking the way they describe the skills they need. People have traditionally labeled abilities like teamwork, adaptability, problem-solving, and communication "soft skills." At the same time, mastery of a specific field like engineering, law, and science has been dubbed mastery of "hard skills."

> *Only 41 percent of CEOs surveyed say they have the people, skills, and resources required to execute their strategies.*

Calling skills "soft" implies they are weak and of little value and low impact, while "hard" suggests toughness, durability, and strength. Since language often reflects how we value things, someone who majored in chemistry at Cornell University probably earns more money than someone who studied history and literature at Vassar college.

Yet the Vassar graduate is more likely to possess the right skills that employers will ultimately need in the future, these so-called "soft skills."[†]

---

[*] https://newsroom.ibm.com/2019-09-06-IBM-Study-The-Skills-Gap-is-Not-a-Myth-But-Can-Be-Addressed-with-Real-Solutions.

[†] For more on how liberal arts degrees are more valuable today, see https://www.ivy-wise.com/ivywise-knowledgebase/resources/article/the-value-of-a-liberal-arts-ed-ucation-in-todays-world/#:~:text=A%20liberal%20arts%20education%20is,the%20individual%20over%20a%20lifetime and https://www.theatlantic.com/

> *The skills of the future are not technical; they're behavioral.*
> —Josh Bersin, global industry analyst

"The skills of the future are not technical; they're behavioral," Josh Bersin, a prominent HR researcher, wrote in his widely read blog.* "Yes, engineers, designers, and technical people need to know how to build and fix things (and we all have to know how to use our computers, tools, and systems at work). However, CEOs and business leaders are now realizing that they can 'buy' these technical skills relatively quickly. It's the soft skills that take effort."

SOFT SKILLS ARE REALLY POWER SKILLS

"These skills are not 'soft'—they're highly complex, take years to learn, and are always changing in their scope," Bersin said. "Take the number one skill CEOs ask for: 'willingness to be flexible, agile, and adaptable to change.' This alone is an enormous bag of personality traits, mindsets, abilities, and experiences."

Bersin suggests we rename soft skills "power skills." I agree.

"These 'power skills' are essential in the world ahead," he said. "Companies like Facebook (which now faces an existential crisis), Amazon (which has become far more extensive than anyone could imagine), Boeing, GE, and many others are not struggling with 'technology strategies.' They are struggling with problems of strategy, ethics, culture, growth, and values." Power skills are what they need most today.

---

education/archive/2017/08/the-unexpected-value-of-the-liberal-arts/535482/.

* https://joshbersin.com/2019/10/lets-stop-talking-about-soft-skills-theyre-power-skills/.

EVALUATING JOB CANDIDATES: A NEW APPROACH

To find employees who possess power skills, companies will need to change their recruiting practices.

Traditionally, a potential employer will examine a candidate's résumé/CV/LinkedIn profile and interview references. But those sources of information only tell employers what the candidate has already done as opposed to what he or she can do or will do. They are backward-looking, and as we know, the future is more relevant than the past when it comes to recruiting. In other words, traditional hiring practices lean toward experience instead of potential.

However, companies are increasingly using technology, including AI, to better predict a candidate's performance. This is how I believe AI should optimally be applied in the future of work—used in a way that helps match employees with better jobs.[*]

For example, Censia, a start-up in San Francisco, uses AI to develop "candidate modeling" in which an employer can search for candidates based on 140 talent attributes.

Censia CEO Joanne Riley had previously founded 1-Page, based on her father's best-selling book, *The One-Page Proposal.* Instead of employers sifting through résumés and references, 1-Page's software allows companies to evaluate and score candidates based on how they solve business problems.

For example, an apparel retailer looking to expand into

---

[*] For more on AI in recruiting, see https://www.vox.com/recode/2019/12/12/20993665/artificial-intelligence-ai-job-screen, https://resources.careerbuilder.com/recruiting-solutions/4-ways-ai-can-enhance-hiring-for-small-businesses, and https://www.forbes.com/sites/forbestechcouncil/2020/07/10/can-ai-improve-your-job-search-it-already-has/#e3c513835277.

China might ask a candidate to submit a one-page plan on how to devise a marketing plan that appeals to local tastes but still offers the cachet of Western brands.

Boston-based Filtered has taken a very novel approach as they have helped top-tier firms around the world hire top technical talent. If you have tried to hire a software engineer in the past twenty years, you know how challenging it can be, and this challenge only seems to be getting tougher. The team at Filtered starts the candidate assessment process by merely having candidates complete a set of assessments. The applicant does not load a résumé/CV/LinkedIn profile, nor do they provide their name, age, gender, or any other identifier. All they do is complete the assessments.

With this highly unbiased data, Filtered can determine the exact technical qualifications of an individual. And this information is produced independent of where they went to school or if they even went to school. The data is also independent of any prior work experience. As CEO Paul Bilodeau told me, "We typically will meet with a new client and ask to see all the candidates they have rejected for positions in the past few months. We approach these individuals and ask them to complete our assessments, and then we map those against some of the hires they have made. Without exception, we have been able to show our clients they are overlooking some exceptional talent due to the way they have designed their recruiting processes and assessments."

This is unique and important. A process that can assess talent quality in a pure form without a bias around age, name, race, gender, school, or company pedigree is extremely valuable. Furthermore, a system that reveals hidden (talent) gems and surfaces high-quality candidates that your normal process rejects or ignores is highly valuable and clearly represents a competitive advantage. A hiring process that removes unconscious bias is also enormously helpful.

IN SEARCH OF ADAPTABILITY: AQ, THE NEW IN-DEMAND SKILL

Some organizations are building processes to measure your agility and adaptability. Consulting giant Deloitte uses immersive online simulations to see how candidates adapt to workplace challenges. The company also looks to hire people who can excel in different roles, industries, or geographies.

"This proves they are agile and a fast learner," said Will Gosling, Deloitte's UK human capital consulting leader.[*]

One emerging attribute organizations are increasingly seeking is something called the adaptability quotient, or AQ. Unlike IQ, which measures intelligence, AQ measures the ability to master new information. It measures how well you spot relevant data, unlearn old information/habits, and demonstrate a commitment to changing how you work.

> *IQ is the minimum you need to get a job, but AQ is how you will be successful over time.*
> —Natalie Fratto, vice president, Goldman Sachs

"IQ is the minimum you need to get a job, but AQ is how you will

---

[*] https://www.bbc.com/worklife/article/20191106-is-aq-more-important-than-intelligence.

be successful over time," said Natalie Fratto,* a New York–based vice president at Goldman Sachs. She became interested in AQ when she was investing in tech start-ups.

AQ focuses on how well employees answer hypothetical what-if questions, a skill you can't measure by looking at a résumé. AQ will be an increasingly visible part of the hiring process going forward. Higher levels of AQ in your company make you more competitive today.

FROM CAREER PATHS TO EMPLOYEE JOURNEYS

"Companies need to take a holistic approach to closing the skills gap . . . that's personalized to the individual and built on data," according to the IBM report. "This means creating educational journeys for employees that are personalized to their current experience level, skills, job role, and career aspirations."

This might require traditional and online training courses, more interactions with other employees from different teams, changing job assignments, and even changing up the physical environments in which employees work.

Employers are increasingly adopting a model called "corpoworking," a play on the coworking spaces popular with freelancers and entrepreneurs. But in corpoworking, the company's employees are the ones who inhabit outside facilities like WeWork offices.

"We've found that these companies and their employees are searching for the same qualities freelancers and entrepreneurs

---

* https://www.bbc.com/worklife/article/20191106-is-aq-more-important-than-intelligence.

report from their experiences in shared workspaces—learning skills faster, making more connections, and feeling inspired and in control," researchers wrote in the *Harvard Business Review*.*

For example, insurance giant Liberty Mutual launched a tech incubator called Solaria Labs. But instead of housing the incubator within the company's offices, Liberty placed Solaria in a WeWork space. The company will also allow non-Solaria employees to use WeWork.

> *We have to learn to shake the many rigid models we've been taught about career paths. They are failing us, and we are falling victim to trying to build organizations around broken and outdated career path models because we* think *employees want them.*

"It allows us to get (access) to new ideas and new talent," said Sandeep Gupta, a vice president and head of innovation at Liberty Mutual. "You can do that pretty easily just rubbing shoulders in the hallway."†

Dozens of companies, ranging from Sprint and AT&T to SAP and IBM, have launched similar experiments.

"The real revolution in coworking may have less to do with freelancers or start-ups than with employees of large companies working beyond the boundaries of their organizations," the *Harvard Business Review* article said.

To advance, employees would typically need to adapt to the company's preset career ladders. But in a realm where employees are not staying as long *and* linear career paths seem

---

*   https://hbr.org/2018/09/why-companies-are-creating-their-own-coworking-spaces.

†   https://www.bizjournals.com/boston/news/2016/01/10/how-liberty-mutual-is-tapping-into-the-start-up.html.

less and less realistic, employers need to rethink their career value proposition. Instead of offering a linear path, perhaps they can provide a diverse set of experiences. Instead of offering, say, a path from marketing analyst to senior marketing analyst to marketing manager, maybe they can offer one from marketing analyst to communications specialist to public relations manager. We have to learn to shake the many rigid models we've been taught about career paths. They are failing us, and we are falling victim to trying to build organizations around broken and outdated career path models because we *think* employees want them. They don't. Today, employees want employers to help them stay relevant, even if that means helping them to a new role outside the organization.

> *Today, employees want employers to help them stay relevant even if that means helping them to a new role outside the organization.*

"We need to give the power back to the employees in order to manage their skill set, their career, and also to face the fact that we have built horribly unhelpful processes like performance reviews and career discussions based on false assumptions that have stifled employee growth and discovery," Philippe Duranton, the Founder and CEO of PhD Talent Accelerator, said. "Many companies are still thinking the old way. Employees don't want intellectual potential career paths. They want to know if there is something available now and what is required to succeed. They want to know what is next and when it will happen."

In summary, if you want to thrive for tomorrow, then you should not just hire for what you need today. The greater adaptability of your employees, the greater the adaptability of your organization. The more you build work in a way that fosters learning, the more you feed the desires of employees to be employable in the future. A learning culture reduces the pressure on recruiting and sets you up for success.

6

THE NEW ORGANIZATION

In earlier chapters we talked about what attributes will define employee success in the future: adaptability, learning velocity, and agility. Interestingly, these same elements form the core of what organizations also need to develop if they are to thrive in the future of work. We are seeing that play out as the world responds to COVID-19 and every company has had to confront a new reality. Creating a more adaptable organization today starts with building a system that will make the organization aware of itself. This requires a high flow of information and intelligence and the ability for anyone in the organization to be able to contribute and withdraw key insights at any hour of the day. In other words, how organizations organize, communicate, and direct traffic to find solutions to new problems can be a significant competitive advantage today.

LEARNING TO FIGHT ZOMBIES

In the 2013 thriller *World War Z*, Brad Pitt plays Gerry Lane, a United Nations investigator searching for the source of a global virus that has turned millions of people into zombies.

He learns that months before the outbreak, officials in Israel had built a protective wall around Jerusalem. As a result, the city was the only place seemingly untouched by the virus and zombies.

Lane traveled to Jerusalem and questioned Jurgen Warmbrunn, the country's top spymaster. How did Israel know?

"We intercepted a communique from an Indian general saying they were fighting the Rakshasha," Warmbrunn said. "Translation, zombies. Technically undead."

Lane wasn't buying it.

"You're Jurgen Warmbrunn, a high-ranking official in the Mossad," Lane said. "Described as sober, efficient, not terribly imaginative. And yet you build a wall because you read a communique that mentions the word 'zombie?'"

Indeed, there was much more to the story. In 1973 Israel disregarded several warnings that Egypt and Syria were about to invade the country. The resulting attack almost eliminated Israel.

As a result, Israel instituted the "tenth man" doctrine: if nine people in the top leadership circle examined the same information and came to the same conclusion, it was the duty of the tenth man to disagree and start planning accordingly, no matter how improbable that outcome.

"Since everyone assumed that this talk of zombies was cover for something else, I began my investigation on the assumption that when they said zombies, they meant zombies," Warmbrunn said.

World War Z is a work of fiction, but the logic behind the tenth man has appeared in some form throughout history.

For example, the beth din was a rabbinical court used extensively in biblical Israel.

In a capital case, if every judge in the beth din found the defendant guilty, the court would set the defendant free. Why? A unanimous court, according to rabbinical law, means a flawed verdict because it suggests the judges did not consider every piece of evidence, especially evidence favorable to the accused.

We usually consider consensus, indeed unanimity, a good thing. If everybody agrees to do or not do something, the decision must be sound, right? How can everybody, especially smart people, be wrong?

Of course, there have been plenty of times in history where consensus has led to bad decisions. The leadership of post–World War I Europe did not think Hitler would do the horrific things he did, despite plenty of evidence to the contrary. Wall Street didn't foresee the great recession, reasoning that the housing bubble was limited to just the subprime mortgage market.

I'm not saying consensus is always wrong. More often than not, the wisdom of many triumphs over the fringe. The question is how we can fully take into account every piece of information, not just the ones we agree with, to make sound decisions.

For companies, answering this question is more critical than ever. With the emergence of new technologies like AI and quantum computing, the economy is changing faster than businesses can adjust.

THE NEED FOR SCENARIO PLANNING

Today I increasingly see more leaders factor in alternatives and potential scenarios on how the competitive landscape might evolve. Employers have had to begin to plan for uncertainty.* Organizations are doing more frequent short-term strategic planning. Instead of sticking to one plan for the entire year, most companies are seeing the need to adjust on the fly, often redoing forecasts midyear. This trend will only accelerate in the years ahead, and clearly COVID-19 has highlighted the critical need for scenario planning. Unfortunately, most of the scenario planning I observe today tends to mostly center around the product, marketing, engineering, or sales strategies. Rarely are organizations considering a wide range of talent strategies to address an increasingly unpredictable future.

What if the United States government changes the rules on or completely halts H-1B visas?†

What if a global pandemic breaks out and everyone is forced to work from home?

What if the available supply of technical talent is so limited in your country that you must recruit and hire talent to work for you in other countries?

What if the skills needed to thrive in your industry change so fast you are incapable of building them at scale?

---

* For more on this topic, read "Leading Through Volatility...Is Your Strategy Ready?," https://www.triumgroup.com/leading-through-volatility-is-your-strategy-ready/.

† The US H-1B visa is a nonimmigrant visa that allows US companies to employ graduate-level workers in specialty occupations that require theoretical or technical expertise in specialized fields such as in IT, finance, accounting, architecture, engineering, mathematics, science, medicine, and the like. Any professional-level job that usually requires you to have a bachelor's degree or higher can come under the H-1B visa for specialty occupations. See https://workpermit.com/immigration/usa/us-h-1b-visa-specialty-workers.

What if you need to manage internships remotely?

These questions and many more need to be thought through as we enter a world where alternative *talent* scenario planning is becoming an imperative.

The challenge of predicting the future is not a lack of information. It's the opposite. Thanks to technology, we're inundated with information. The real problem is how we can design an organization to accomplish three things:

- accumulate diverse sources of information
- share that information with the right people
- create a culture that embraces ambiguity and gives equal weight to both consensual and contrarian information

In other words, companies need to build an organization that incorporates the tenth man doctrine, one that avoids group thinking. One that allows businesses to adapt to a fast-changing economy by incorporating all information—even the information we might instinctively find uncomfortable, unlikely, or downright crazy.

ACCUMULATING DIVERSE SOURCES OF INFORMATION

Perhaps the most obvious way of avoiding groupthink is to solicit information from outside company walls. That sounds like a no-brainer, but often companies who have been successful in the past will stick to their previous methods. After all, if it's not broken, then don't fix it, right?

The problem is that business models and market conditions

today can abruptly change. In previous chapters we reviewed the fact that employees should build networks that include both personal and professional interests. Similarly, employers need to construct broad ecosystems of information from alumni, partners, customers, and even competitors.

Collaborating with competitors is one key reason why Silicon Valley is what it is today.

> *Collaborating with competitors is one key reason why Silicon Valley is what it is today.*

Back in the 1960s, Boston could have become the top tech incubator in the United States. After all, it was home to research universities like Harvard and MIT and early major tech firms like Wang Laboratories and Digital Equipment.

However, in her book *Regional Advantage*, author Annalee Saxenian argues Silicon Valley ultimately emerged as tech's epicenter because it created a culture in which companies and entrepreneurs actively shared information beyond corporate boundaries. Such open networks more quickly facilitated the movement of ideas compared to other places like the East Coast.

Take Tesla. The electric car maker realized the biggest obstacle to its growth wasn't traditional auto manufacturers like Ford and General Motors but instead weak consumer demand for electric vehicles. So CEO Elon Musk realized he first needed to expand the size of the overall market.

So, in 2019 Tesla gave away its patents to other automakers so they too could build cars that could attract consumer interest.*

---

* https://www.ndtv.com/world-news/elon-musk-releases-all-tesla-patents-to-help-save-the-earth-1986450#:~:text=Elon%20Musk%20announced%20Thursday%20

Musk realized that hoarding information on electric vehicles would consign Tesla to the status of a fringe player in the auto industry. In other words, Tesla realized that its most significant barrier to growth was not another car manufacturer; it was the public's adoption of electric vehicles. It needed other car makers to build electric cars. And in another stroke of genius, Tesla announced it was making a global grid of charging stations. Hence, as the market picked up, it would have another revenue stream.

Companies, especially retailers, are also increasingly operating "test stores" or showrooms to gather intelligence about consumer preferences. Target, the nation's second-largest retailer, has an innovation center in San Francisco where it regularly meets with start-ups to see their new products. Also, many malls and cities around the world are experimenting with so-called "pop-up shops" as a new form of retail experience.*

Another approach to building more diverse sources of intelligence is being intentional about immersing your leaders in different experiences *outside* of your company. This is the main focus of Wavelength, a leading-edge, immersive leadership company based in the UK. Adrian Simpson, who is a co-founder of Wavelength, put it this way:

"Many long-established organizations face a challenge in that they often have leaders with long tenure and very little understanding of how other companies innovate or indeed operate. Moreover, they are consumed by solving issues in their firm and don't take time to press the pause button, look outside, observe, question, probe, and debate. This is where we come in.

"We provide leaders with insider access to the boardrooms

---

he,wants%20to%20use%20our%20technology.%22.

*   https://www.bloomberg.com/news/articles/2007-02-09/pop-up-stores-all-the-ragebusinessweek-business-news-stock-market-and-financial-advice.

and shop floors of some of the world's most admired, success-ful, and innovative companies. The cohorts are sometimes made of entire exec teams or more frequently of leaders from differ-ent geographies, industries, and sectors who learn alongside and from each other.

"This combination of inspiration, education, and indeed provocation provides them with the awareness and impetus to effect change."

Client after client has told Simpson how much their eyes have been opened to new possibilities by stepping out of their routines with Wavelength. "At Wavelength, this is what we call ROI—Re-turn on Inspiration," Simpson said. "We want to facilitate the exposure of leaders to world-class people and ideas." And this is crucial for organizations today. In a world that is changing fast, exposing your leaders to ideas, people, and insights outside the walls of your organization is enormously valuable.

A further benefit to the way Wavelength works is that a premium is placed on building your network when you are enrolled in any of their programs. Simpson is the person who introduced me to Zella King and Amanda Scott many years ago, and he invites them to present the Personal Boardroom idea to his clients. As discussed earlier, networking is a critical skill for employees to develop. Unfortunately, most employers focus on building networks for their employees *inside* the firm and miss the opportunity to grow networks *outside*. Wavelength offers us an elegant model that combines learning with intentional net-working outside the organization.

GROWING YOUR EMPLOYEE NETWORKS

The recognition that networking is so crucial to early-stage organizations has led to many leading venture capital* (often referred to as VC) and private equity† firms, as well as start-up incubators, to create positions in their firms where people focus 100 percent of their time on helping entrepreneurs in the portfolio grow their networks. They introduce leaders in their portfolio to high-quality talent, advisers, mentors, and board members. Andreessen-Horowitz, one of the most well-known VCs in Silicon Valley, has a whole team dedicated to helping its portfolio companies and leaders find people who can help them. They are not recruiters—they are purely network builders and connectors.

John Hill is a networking ninja and someone I got to know when we worked together at LinkedIn. Today, John is the VP of

---

* According to Investopedia, "Venture capital is a form of private equity and a type of financing that investors provide to start-up companies and small businesses that are believed to have long-term growth potential. Venture capital generally comes from well-off investors, investment banks, and any other financial institutions. However, it does not always take a monetary form; it can also be provided in the form of technical or managerial expertise. Venture capital is typically allocated to small companies with exceptional growth potential, or to companies that have grown quickly and appear poised to continue to expand." https://www.investopedia.com/terms/v/venturecapital.asp

† Investopedia explains, "Private equity, at its most basic, is equity—shares representing ownership of, or an interest in, an entity—that is not publicly listed or traded. Private equity is a source of investment capital from high-net-worth individuals and firms. These investors buy shares of private companies—or gain control of public companies with the intention of taking them private and ultimately delisting them from public stock exchanges. Large institutional investors dominate the private equity world, including pension funds and large private equity firms funded by a group of accredited investors." https://www.investopedia.com/terms/p/privateequity.asp

network at Techstars, a leading worldwide start-up ecosystem that helps entrepreneurs succeed. John's primary job is to accelerate the growth and vitality of the networks of the leaders in the Techstars community. I love how Hill puts it: "The founders I work with are incredible atoms. It's my role to get them to collide."

> *The founders I work with are incredible atoms. It's my role to get them to collide.*
> —John Hill, VP of Network, Techstars

Dan Portillo is yet another master connector. He is the managing partner for a new services-based venture fund called Sweat Equity Ventures, which takes the operating VC model to a whole new level. Rather than capital, Sweat Equity Ventures invests its operational expertise in product, engineering, and go-to-market strategy in exchange for equity.* They leverage their network to build products, acquire customers, and recruit key employees. This is a very novel approach but a testament to just how powerful and valuable networks can be.

Hill and Portillo are great examples of the necessity of being intentional with networking, especially when tackling a new venture. Doing new things is challenging, and the more diversity of people and ideas you have surrounding you, the more likely you will be able to navigate through it.

Intentional external networking is not a role that I have seen

---

* According to Investopedia, "Equity, typically referred to as shareholders' equity (or owners' equity for privately held companies), represents the amount of money that would be returned to a company's shareholders if all of the assets were liquidated and all of the company's debt was paid off."
https://www.investopedia.com/terms/e/equity.asp.

sit within most employers outside of the VC, private equity, and start-up incubator communities. I strongly encourage employers to help grow the networks of their teams outside of company walls. This is a critical talent strategy for today.

SHARING THE RIGHT INFORMATION WITH THE RIGHT PEOPLE

Target had to learn the hard way that it needed better ways to receive and share information.

On an early September morning in 2011, millions of consumers logged onto Target.com eagerly looking to buy clothing and handbags from Missoni. The venerable Italian design house had partnered with Target to create the retailer's most ambitious, exclusive, limited-time merchandise assortment.

Instead, consumers were greeted with a message that Target.com was down. So many people had flooded the website that it had crashed and remained dark for most of the day. And the consumers who were able to get through soon discovered that the retailer didn't correctly process their orders. In some cases, Target took their money but had no record of the transaction.

How did Target, one of the country's most respected retailers, mess up this vital moment?

Before the debacle Target had made a big decision. After years of outsourcing its website operations to Amazon, the company decided to take back control of Target.com and completely redesign it. Target rolled out the new website in August 2011, a month before it would launch its collaboration with Missoni.

Any competent IT person, however, would tell you that a company just can't redesign a site and then flip on a switch and say, "Ta-da!" A website as complex as Target.com only a few weeks away from a significant merchandise launch would require several months of "load testing" to see if the website could handle such traffic and to correct any software bugs.

Unfortunately, the person who would be in the best position to know this information, the actual head of Target.com, was far removed from the senior leadership circle on the corporate hierarchy. He wasn't even a vice president. In a culture dominated by merchandisers and marketers, no one thought that the person who directly oversaw Target's e-commerce business was important enough to attend the same meetings as the CEO.

Companies that do not effectively share information face severe consequences, especially in an era of fast-shifting changes. The average US large business loses $47 million a year because it can't distribute information well, according to a report by Panopto and YouGov.[*] Also, employees waste 5.3 hours every week either waiting for vital information from their colleagues or working to recreate existing institutional knowledge.

"It's an expensive oversight," the report said. "Employees are wasting time, and companies are losing money. Institutional knowledge is valuable, and it's frustrating for employees when an answer isn't available when it's needed. Unshared expertise costs companies millions of dollars that could be put to better use."

---

[*]   https://www.prnewswire.com/news-releases/inefficient-knowledge-sharing-costs-large-businesses-47-million-per-year-300681971.html.

THE CASE FOR HYPER AWARENESS

One organization is focused entirely on helping companies gather valuable insights from employees and, in some cases, from partners and customers.

Waggl, founded in 2014 and based in Sausalito, California, offers a unique platform that disrupts the traditional employee survey. The company's real-time technology allows employees to rank the responses of coworkers whose answers were more accurate, relevant, or on point than those of others. While most employee surveys collect insights from the employees, rarely do companies share what other employees are thinking and saying, let alone have them vote on/crowdsource the most insightful comments. Waggl's design elevates the employee survey to something far more useful and valuable. The organization is learning from itself rather than just having management read the survey results and report out to the company what they think they should hear. This may explain why Waggl is thriving, was recently ranked 151 on the 2019 *Inc.* 5000 list, and why they are consistently voted a "best place to work."

> *While most employee surveys collect insights from the employees, rarely do companies share what other employees are thinking and saying, let alone have them vote on the most insightful comments.*

"Waggl is the most human way for organizations to crowdsource feedback and create connection and surface actionable insight," CEO Michael Papay said. The platform "helps clients cultivate internal hyperawareness and agility in order to make more informed decisions and execute faster."*

---

*   https://www.hrtechnologist.com/interviews/employee-engagement/making-work-more-human-in-conversation-with-michael-papay-cofounder-and-ceo-at-waggl/.

This increased necessity for firms to become hyperaware of critical issues in a dynamic, continually changing reality cannot be overstated. Another firm doing pioneering work in the world of identifying employee sentiment is Emtrain. Based in San Francisco, California, Emtrain's original focus was creating high-caliber online compliance training. Over time Emtrain realized it could identify the root causes of cultural issues within its compliance training. They also realized they could diagnose and benchmark employee sentiment regarding those root culture issues so stakeholders and organizations could address the disease rather than the symptoms. This allowed them to improve workplace culture measurably. Rather than delivering one-dimensional, passive content, Emtrain started providing multidimensional content that integrates diagnostic questions such as:

- "Do your managers understand the implications of their power on direct reports?"
- "Do the coworkers on your team have strong social intelligence skills?"

Emtrain pivoted from a traditional training firm to a software and analytics company that provides clients precious cultural insights about their own workplace culture. Today Emtrain can offer a process to organizations that not only surfaces highly sensitive topics but also does so in a safe, constructive manner. Its services are accompanied by expert advice and support. Emtrain helps employees learn how to work through difficult situations, and it helps organizations and leaders address these matters proactively and strategically.

In a world of constant change where misunderstandings seem to be more frequent, a system that helps everyone work through difficult issues is extremely valuable. It's an essential part of a healthy culture. Training that is designed to learn from the participants and feed these insights back into the system to make it better is brilliant. It turns your basic training into a company improvement exercise.

> *In a world of constant change where misunderstandings seem to be more frequent, a system that helps everyone work through difficult issues is extremely valuable. It's an essential part of a healthy culture.*

LEVERAGING YOUR BOARD OF DIRECTORS

Ensuring the right information is in the hands of the right people starts at the top with the board of directors.

Boards can often be passive entities, often deferring to the CEO, who frequently also serves as chairman. That's why it's crucial for companies to recruit and empower independent directors.

According to the BCG Henderson Institute, "Given directors' other responsibilities and the infrequent nature of board meetings, it is challenging for them to stay up to date on key trends and continuously validate the firm's strategic direction."[*]

"A robust knowledge system can give directors the information they need," the institute said. "Frequent updates should keep directors apprised of changes in the environment and resulting impacts on firm strategy. And directors should have access to a repository of on-demand materials to increase their

---

[*] https://bcghendersoninstitute.com/the-boards-role-in-strategy-in-a-changing-environment-ec143e7ec558.

inside knowledge of the company."

In June 2017 Target chairman and CEO Brian Cornell was on a plane when Amazon declared its intention to pay $13.7 billion to purchase Whole Foods Market. By the time Cornell landed, his phone was inundated with messages about the megadeal, including breathless headlines that declared the death of physical retail.

Typically boards only meet four times a year. But Cornell arranged for a conference call with the board of directors to discuss the situation. After all, Target stock, along with that of other brick-and-mortar retailers, lost billions of dollars in market value shortly after Amazon announced the deal.

"It was the topic of conversation everywhere across the country," Cornell told the annual Stanford Directors' College in Palo Alto.* "People are sitting at dinner and asking what just happened, and what does it mean?"

The BCG Henderson Institute recommends boards regularly invite outside experts to meetings. Some boards even boast special committees of directors that focus on potential disruptions to the business. In a way, this is an invitation for a tenth man to join boardroom debates.

Even CEOs, those who hold the most powerful position at a company, need to make an extra effort to get information, especially if the business is a large and complex one where information is tightly controlled from top to bottom, and vice versa.

When Rex Geveden became CEO of BWX Technologies in 2017, he knew that several of his executives were former military leaders who strongly believed in a chain of command. That meant that they were trained only to speak to their immediate superior, not anyone above him or her.

---

*   https://www.sfchronicle.com/business/article/Target-CEO-to-Amazon-Bring-it-11260258.php.

But when it came to sharing information, Geveden made it clear that he didn't believe in such a system.

"I warned them, I'm going to communicate with all levels of the organization down to the shop floor, and you can't feel paranoid or suspicious about that," Geveden said. "I told them that I would not interfere with your decisions that belong in your chain of command, but I will give and receive information anywhere in the organization, at any time.

"I just can't get enough understanding of the organization from listening to the voices at the top," he said.*

Geveden's approach is similar to the idea of "circular management." Instead of a hierarchical ladder, the CEO sits at the circle's center, and information can flow in many different directions.

"Anyone in the circle had numerous entry points to communicate with anyone in the next circle, rather than just a single superior who acted as a gate," he explained.†

Your board of directors can serve as the tenth man to your firm, or it can be a check in the box on compliance and governance. If you truly want to leverage the treasures of your board, first make sure you have the right people on the board, and then confirm the frequency of meetings fits the realities of your business. Then verify that their access to your organization information consists of more than a PowerPoint dump once a quarter.

---

*   David Epstein, *Range: Why Generalists Triumph in a Specialized World* (New York: Riverhead Books, 2019), 264.

†   Epstein, 264.

ITERATION AND EXPERIMENTATION: THE LINKEDIN EXECUTIVE STAFF MEETING

During my years at LinkedIn, we spent a great deal of time thinking through how we wanted to run the company. We debated how we wanted to organize and communicate and how we wanted to make decisions, among other things. When it came to the guts of the business—as is the case in most organizations— the executive staff was the place all critical decisions were made.

We experimented with at least twenty different ways of running the company:

- What was the best day and time of the week to meet?
- How long should the meeting run?
- What is the best data to review before and during the meeting?
- Who should be invited to the meeting?
- Who would own the agenda?
- What topics were most important to discuss, and in what order?
- How do we make sure the remote and international locations are "plugged in?"

We iterated, iterated, and iterated. One week we would try having every exec give a status report, and then the next we would try having only a few topics discussed with no report outs, and so on. At the time I was very frustrated with all these constant changes, as I had been used to working in large systems that had well-worn operational paths. I'd never been part of building the operational rhythm of a business. It was way harder than I had realized. I didn't recognize how valuable that experimentation process would become.

In the end, after almost two years of experimenting, we settled on a framework that worked really well. We met as an executive team of, say, twelve or thirteen top leaders who reported to the CEO, Jeff Weiner, every Tuesday for four hours. Jeff owned the agenda, but we appointed a project manager (PM) for this meeting to help us keep on task and to free Jeff up to participate versus worry about logistics.

By Friday of every week, we had to submit data to the PM for the meeting. We listed the company's top priorities and ranked them from one to fifty. Every project featured a description and a color-coded system of its status: red for trouble, yellow for some warning signs, and green for on track.

We reviewed three simple parts on every project:

1. Did they have the right leadership on the project?
2. Did the project team have the right level of staffing and resources?
3. Was the project on track and meeting its goals?

For every project with a red or yellow status, we built action plans and assigned owners to fix the problems. We had a clear visual dashboard of every priority in the company, and most projects intersected with other members of the team. For example, if a project was too low on resources, I would jump in to discuss a game plan as the head of talent. It was terrific.

Every meeting would begin with a review of the top-priority project in the company. We did not move to the second priority until we had ensured everything was green or that we had a plan to make it green. This ensured the most critical projects got the most attention first, and if they were on track, we just moved down the priority list one by one.

The system served us well because it created a sense of shared awareness and accountability among all of the executives, no matter their department. We all tried to help one another, and most importantly, we spent time on the topics that mattered the most to the company. It also assured that the usual arguments for resources were focused on the right priorities. If Project 10 and Project 50 were both short three people, the former would receive the extra help over the latter.

Now, I'm not here to tell you that this method was perfect or that it is right for your organization. Instead, I want to show you the process of how we arrived at a highly functioning model for our team. We tried, experimented, learned, continuously adjusted, and then settled upon a way that helped us run the company. I'd be surprised if LinkedIn still used that exact format today as iteration and change are necessary as a company changes and leaders change. What works for some does not work for all, but experimentation is the key to unlocking the best methods. And a process that all your leaders build together by design facilitates deep adoption and buy-in.

BUILDING THE TENTH-MAN CULTURE

Collecting and distributing information is vital. But the will to absorb and use it, especially when it comes to contrarian information, is a lot harder to do.

That's because typical corporate cultures ignore or even discourage dissent and contrarian thinking. People don't want to speak their minds because they feel doing so will only make them look bad or potentially hurt their careers.

Take Target. For most of its nearly sixty-year history, the company only hired CEOs and top leaders from within, employees who had risen through the ranks steeped in the "Target way." To succeed at the retailer, employees needed to swear absolute fidelity to the "Target way."

The system created a culture of consistency and stability but also one of groupthink, especially when things went wrong, like in the Missoni debacle.

When Target debuted in Canada in 2013, its first week was marred by poor inventory planning: stores ran out of basic merchandise like bread and milk. Despite multiple news reports and a tsunami of consumer complaints, which were amplified by social media, the company continued to deny any systemic problems. Two years later, Target pulled out of Canada and reported a $2.1 billion loss.

Inventory shortages are no small problem, and surely someone at Target must have been aware of them. But that news never reached top executives, or perhaps they failed to believe it. Target leaders were acutely averse to negative information, which only discouraged anyone from delivering the bad news. When everyone says things are going well, no one wants to listen to the one person who says otherwise.

To build a culture that can adapt to changing circumstances, businesses need to design ways to encourage employees to push back against the consensus or the "company way." This is increasingly an imperative today.

> *To build a culture that can truly adapt to changing circumstances, businesses need to design ways to encourage employees to push back against the consensus or the "company way."*

Culture can actually be too internally consistent. The experiments have shown that an effective problem-solving culture was one that balanced standard practice—whatever it happened to be—with forces that pushed in the opposite direction.

If managers were used to process conformity, encouraging individualism helped them to employ "ambidextrous thought" and learn what worked in each situation. The trick was expanding the organization's range by identifying the dominant culture and then diversifying it by pushing in the opposite direction.*

Here are three examples of how companies pushed the other way.

Toyota: Executives at the automaker deliberately set broad goals in order to force people from across departments to work together to meet them.

"If [the CEO] makes [the goal] more concrete, employees won't be able to exercise their full potential," said Zenji Yasuda, a former Toyota senior managing director. "The vague nature of this goal confers freedom to researchers to open new avenues of exploration; procurement to look for new and unknown suppliers who possess needed technology, and sales to consider the next steps needed to sell such products."†

Another way Toyota sought to push departments to collaborate was to set seemingly overambitious goals.

In 1993 design teams working on the Prius created a prototype that offered a 50 percent boost in fuel efficiency over existing models. But executives demanded a 100 percent improvement. The teams knew they couldn't achieve such a feat with existing gasoline-based technologies. The problem forced

---

* Epstein, 257.

† https://hbr.org/2008/06/the-contradictions-that-drive-toyotas-success.

the team to ask Toyota's research and development lab for help. The result was a hybrid electric/gasoline engine.

Siemens: The German manufacturing conglomerate created a system called ShareNet, a network where people from sales, marketing, and development departments can access best practices based on the combined experiences of seven thousand employees in fifty countries across the world.

"ShareNet covers both explicit and tacit, but always experience-based, knowledge of the sales value creation process including project know-how, technical and functional solution components, and the business environment (e.g., customer, competitor, market, and partner knowledge). In addition, ShareNet provides less structured spaces such as chats, community news, discussion groups on special issues, and so-called 'urgent requests.' As ShareNet works independent of time zones and organizational boundaries, members usually get answers to 'urgent requests' within a few hours."*

To encourage people to use it, Siemens offered "reward points" to employees who could document how they used the information to solve a problem.

"Leaders should be encouraging employees to seek and share experiences often," said Christopher Myers, an assistant professor at the Johns Hopkins University Carey Business School and Armstrong Institute for Patient Safety and Quality.

"This gives individuals license to seek out what they need to learn, without fear that they're intrusive or bothersome— or that it will make them look bad," Myers said. "People often hesitate to ask others for help or advice because it requires ad-

---

*   http://ceur-ws.org/Vol-37/Doering.pdf.

mitting they don't know something important. So instead, they work in isolation, redoing something that their colleagues may have already done or making similar mistakes."*

More incentives: Michael Schrage, a research fellow at the MIT Sloan School's Center for Digital Business, said he consulted for a large company struggling to get employees to communicate information and share ideas.

"Leadership recognized that business units and functions had effectively been allowed to ignore the rest of the enterprise," Schrage said. "Significant opportunities and resources were left underexplored or untouched."†

So, Schrage helped the company create two complementary contests. The first was called "Thief of the Month," which recognized an employee who had "stolen" an idea or innovation from another department and used it to improve their own business. The second contest, dubbed "We Wuz Robbed," rewarded a department whose practices had been successfully adopted by another internal group.

"Dual prizes created a symmetrical 'marketplace' where employees were simultaneously encouraged not just to look for interesting ideas to 'steal' but to think about which of their own best practices deserved wider internal promotion," Schrage said. "The competition thus incented both 'supply' and 'demand' of knowledge worth sharing."

By casting a broad net for input and opinions, companies stand a higher chance of incorporating contrarian, unlikely, or even unpleasant information into their strategic thinking. As a

---

* https://hbr.org/2015/11/is-your-company-encouraging-employees-to-share-what-they-know.

† https://hbr.org/2012/12/a-simpler-way-to-get-employees-to-share.html.

result, they will be much more prepared to adapt to an increasingly unpredictable economy and marketplace.

THE ECOSYSTEM MODEL

Another way of thinking about the company of the future is to think in terms of an organization as an ecosystem. Networks can help an individual expand their access to information and opportunities, and an ecosystem model presents a similar benefit for an organization. If you extend your traditional view of a company and combine it with the lessons that Saxenian discussed, you start to shape a compelling new model. Ecosystems are generally more open than closed systems and offer more leverage and increased diversity of ideas and perspectives.

ISDI Digital University,* founded in Madrid, Spain, in 2009, is an excellent example of the merits of an ecosystem model. What began as a digital business class in a small, rented room in Madrid turned into a leading global digital transformation ecosystem, reaching thousands of students and business leaders across the globe. ISDI presents a compelling model of how an organization can be built in a way that draws as much value from the outside as it does from the inside.

ISDI creates a curriculum through its global teachers. These teachers are all highly active business leaders at companies such as Google, Amazon, eBay, LinkedIn, Facebook, Salesforce, and Airbnb. Every teacher at ISDI teaches after their day job, and this allows them to bring freshness and relevance to the topics that matter today. This ensures that students are learning what is

---

* ISDI is an abbreviation for Instituto Superior para el Desarrollo de Internet (Higher Institute for Internet Development).

current, necessary, and practical. While ISDI offers many classes, degrees, and certifications, the core offering at ISDI is what is known as an MIB—master of internet business—degree. What distinguishes the MIB experience is that over the course of the nine-month program, you are asked to apply everything you learn in classes into what is known as a "backbone project." This backbone project requires that you propose to digitally transform a real local business. The practical application of learning is applied to local businesses who are interested in digitally transforming themselves—contributing to a virtuous system whereby the school not only is building digital talent but also helping many firms transform along the way.

This work by students in the business community has led to a growing demand for ISDI to help businesses digitally transform—expanding the ecosystem to include what ISDI calls "in-company." And as you can imagine, the work ISDI performs in firms around the world provides it with insights into what skills individuals and companies need to develop. It also learns what challenges digital transformation is presenting to organizations that it can help address, which in turn helps it build a better curriculum.

The ecosystem model works to ISDI's advantage in so many ways. Students invite ISDI into their companies, the knowledge they gain improves the curriculum, and the in-company surfaces more students. The school naturally improves itself while adding value to the communities it serves.

As ISDI began to grow, its open structure and approach surfaced yet another new opportunity. Many students were not only interested in improving their digital business acumen so that they could be more effective in their firm but also were so enamored with the possibilities that ISDI was helping them reveal that they wanted help launching their own start-ups. Thus, ISDI's IMPACT Accelerator was created, and in a short time, it has become the leading accelerator in Spain and one of the top five public business accelerators in the world.*

Since 2009, ISDI has expanded to the point that some of the graduates are now professors, start-up founders, or, in some cases, even investors in other ISDI-supported ventures. The ecosystem model facilitates all of this opportunity. Beyond just business, in its work with so many students and business leaders, ISDI has identified many nonprofit, community-oriented projects where it could also make an impact. Today, it is working on a massive global project with UNICEF.

From the very start, ISDI strove to be a versatile digital entity, which led it to invest heavily in building its online resources: digital library, e-learning courses, webinar archive, and so on. These vast digital resources allowed it to experiment and create more engaging online content. ISDI regularly experiments with different forms of online learning, continually striving to build a model that is always learning, evolving, adapting, and improving. And this is a crucial point, as co-founders CEO Nacho de Pinedo and President Javier Zapatero point out: "Our goal was not to just build a specific school but rather to build a learning system that constantly grows, changes, adjusts, and is at the front of what individuals, organizations, and societies need most. We did not have a master plan to become an ecosystem, but as we grew, we realized this was our destiny, and the ecosystem model has been a key element of our success. This is the digital reality of business and education today. It is all about continual transformation."

---

*   https://www.impact-accelerator.com/isdi-accelerator-ranked-world-top-5-public-business-accelerator/.

> *We did not have a master plan to become an ecosystem, but as we grew, we realized this was our destiny, and the ecosystem model has been a key element of our success. This is the digital reality of business and education today. It is all about continual transformation.*
>
> —Nacho de Pinedo and Javier Zapatero,
> co-founders, ISDI

The ecosystem model paired with its deep investments in digital online learning assets allowed ISDI, unlike most universities in the world, to immediately pivot and continue to thrive when the coronavirus pandemic forced schools to close their doors. The ISDI model is an excellent example for organizations to draw from today. Built as an ecosystem that tightly connects to the marketplace and the needs of students, ISDI has developed an excellent template for other organizations to follow.

ISDI did not create the ecosystem model, nor did it set out to build that model from the start. Yet it came to realize it was a valuable model that has allowed it in a few short years to achieve tremendous success. This framework has allowed it to turn insights into action quickly. And a small administration allows for fast learning and transfer of information, so the team is always sharing and connected.

In today's unpredictable and fast-changing world of commerce, having a model that allows you to learn and pivot quickly is essential. A model that will enable you to listen to your customers, your employees, your board, and your tenth man sets you up for optimal adaptability and puts you more in control of your future.

Plus, it will help you ward off those zombies!

CONCLUSION

NO TIME LIKE THE PRESENT

I first started to write this book in early 2019, which, in hindsight, seems like an entire generation ago. At the time, the US economy was still expanding, unemployment was low, and the stock market was booming.

Despite these positive indicators, I wanted employees and employers to take the long view, to realize that technology was changing the economy faster than anyone had expected and that we needed to prepare ourselves for the unknown.

Well, the unknown has arrived. As I pen these paragraphs, the COVID-19 virus has killed over a million people globally, including four hundred thousand Americans, and has shut down society at large. Millions of people are out of work, businesses have filed for bankruptcy, and the economy is only at the start of a painful recession.

Few people, including me, could have predicted such a catastrophe. The world will no doubt emerge from this pandemic permanently changed in many respects.

But the lessons from this book are still relevant, if not more so. In fact, the pandemic may only speed up the changes in our economy and society that technology has already unleashed.

Whether unemployed or forced to work at home, employees have had to adapt to rapid changes in circumstances. Homes became offices and classrooms literally overnight for much of the world. Side hustles, networking, and online learning are more essential than ever.

For companies, the need to adapt on the fly, collect information, distribute it to the right people, and explore different scenarios and options is crucial to their survival.

We've already seen companies, whether small businesses or large corporations, do this.

In Memphis, City Tasting Tours decided to partner with local restaurants to create new foods and then deliver them to customers along with a link to a thirty-minute video about the food, restaurants, and the city. Castalia at Sfumato in Detroit went from operating a scent shop to delivering frozen juice cubes that, when added to spirits, become homemade cocktails.[*]

Large manufacturers like General Motors, Tesla, and Ford have converted their assembly lines in order to make ventilators and other equipment for hospital staff. Retailers like Target and Best Buy ramped up their e-commerce operations when stay-at-home orders shut down physical stores.

Universities and their students have turned to ingenuity to cope with COVID-19. For example, students at the University of California at Berkeley have used the popular video game platform Minecraft to build a completely digital version of the

---

[*]   https://www.nytimes.com/2020/04/23/business/coronavirus-small-businesses-adapt.html.

physical campus. They plan to use the technology to offer virtual tours to incoming freshmen, host online commencement ceremonies, and even produce a digital musical to raise money for coronavirus relief efforts.

WITNESS THE ULTIMATE LEADERSHIP TEST

If you are seeking a job today, the prospects may feel grim as the supply of open positions has disappeared and many thousands of people have lost their jobs. But if you step back for a moment, there are some significant advantages for all of us when we consider the future of work and the future of careers. First, every one of us is learning how to be more adaptable and more agile in every sphere of our lives. COVID-19 has forced us all to live differently in addition to working differently. Over the long term, this can only improve our ability to become more adaptable and resilient. Second, from an employee perspective, the pandemic has provided us the ultimate leadership scorecard. In our lifetimes and for all generations alive today, we have never seen a leadership test of this scale and magnitude testing leaders, executives, organizations, countries, states, and cultures far and wide.

We can see during this global crisis:

- Who is stepping up as a leader?
- Which organizations have quickly learned to adapt?
- Which employers are helping their communities?
- Which leaders are conspicuously silent?
- Which companies are taking advantage of the pandemic to try and reap more profits for themselves?

This data is enormously helpful so that when jobs do start returning, you will know more about which organizations are worthy of your talents.

In chapter 3 I wrote about the scooter industry and how Bird was the fastest company in history to reach unicorn status. I also mentioned that the lack of leadership and industry depth was not something that caused many candidates to hesitate about joining their firm. Well, sadly, Bird demonstrated during the pandemic what can happen during a crisis when you have untested leadership. In late March 2020, Bird notified over four hundred staff via a prerecorded message by an unknown, faceless individual that played on a Zoom call that their jobs were being eliminated. No CEO was present. No executive spoke on the call to employees. No executive demonstrated any ownership. Instead, a Wizard of Oz curtain was dropped by management so they could hide behind their lawyers and have someone else give the bad news. Fail. As one of the notified employees said, "It felt like a *Black Mirror* episode."* It was a case study in poor leadership. Do you think future applicants to Bird will take note of this? You bet they will.

Around the same time, another unicorn, Airbnb, let 24 percent of its workforce go due to the pandemic. But the way it conducted the process set the gold standard for how leadership can manage staff reductions in a way that builds loyalty even among those leaving. It led the staff reduction in a way that took the long view of its relationship with the departing and remaining employees. As *Business Insider* put it, the way Airbnb conducted its staff reductions was "a prime example of how to

---

* https://dot.la/bird-layoffs-meeting-story-2645612465.html

do layoffs right, in a way that's respectful, compassionate, and pragmatic."* Among other things, Airbnb converted all its recruiters into job agents for the employees being let go. It built a database filled with all the departing employees to share with other companies to make its impacted employees more marketable and easier to find. It bent the rules for stock vesting, so even if you were with the company less than a year, you would receive a full year of stock vesting. It did things most companies never do in a layoff. That extra effort for its departing staff lit up on Twitter, Facebook, and LinkedIn with glowing stories of the people who were let go raving about their experiences at Airbnb and mourning having to leave such a great culture. Many of the Airbnb employees who did not lose their jobs reached out to their networks to help place their departing colleagues. Airbnb did it right. Bird did it wrong. These examples are but a few of the many insights we have gleaned as one organization after another, and one leader after another, shows its true colors during this global crisis.

OUR LEADERSHIP MOMENT

This is our leadership moment. Right now. Today. Now is the time to tackle the most significant challenges and changes in your career journey or your organization. The environment is ripe for change because everyone already has to do so many things in life differently. The table is set. Now is the time for us to build a better model for the employer-employee relationship. One that both parties believe fits today's realities rather than

---

*   https://www.businessinsider.com/airbnb-ceo-brian-chesky-layoffs-show-respect-compassion-for-employees-2020-5.

one that uses outdated foundations and practices. We need a better, more honest, more realistic compact between the two camps. This book intends to ignite ideas we can build into a more satisfying model for the future of work together.

While every employer will likely tweak their model to fit their circumstances, market, and business, the elements that need to be considered to create a successful one have been laid out in this book. The exact employer model that will inspire you as an employee will vary and depend on your unique needs, values, and aspirations. There is no one right model for every employer, just as not every employee looks at work similarly. Still, we know we need a better one than most of what is out there today, and this book presents the ingredients. It's now up to you to make the right recipe for you, your career, and your organization.

We will need more enlightened leadership to look up and see this as an increasingly complex world where old models of long tenure and Tony Soprano HR policies do more harm than good. We will need employers to build cultures that inspire people to do their best work even after they leave. We will need employers to see they can build value from beyond just their employees, leveraging alumni and gig workers and creating reinforcing ecosystems. We will need employees to recognize that growth can happen in many forms within an enterprise, and sometimes running to the next hot company might not produce the learning and growth you desire. We will need employees to understand that employers are confused too and as unsure of the future as they are.

DISRUPTION CREATES OPPORTUNITIES

While it may not feel like it today, many great things can come out of challenging circumstances and periods of chaos and disruption. During the last global recession in 2007, when many banks faced collapse and thousands lost their jobs and their homes, many highly successful companies were born that are thriving today. Some of the well-known companies that were founded between 2007 and 2009 include Instagram, Pinterest, WhatsApp, Glassdoor, Venmo, Box, Uber, Airbnb, Slack, and Beats. That's right—all of these companies were born in a very dark economic climate.

Rahm Emanuel, the former mayor of Chicago who served as in President Obama's chief of staff, was famous for saying, "Never let a serious crisis go to waste. And what I mean by that is, it's an opportunity to do things you think you could not do before."[*] We need to seize this opportunity.

Tim Harford is a man who has studied how frustration and chaos can make us more creative. In 2016 he gave a fabulous TED Talk on this subject.[†] In it Harford explains, "I think we have to gain an appreciation for the unexpected advantages of having to cope with a little mess." In difficult times. Harford explains, we slow down, we focus more, we get a bit more intense, and, consequently, we learn more. We can unlock a creative reservoir we don't usually access.

---

[*] https://mattermark.com/2007-2009-financial-crisis-surprisingly-kind-tech-start-ups/. Note that Emanuel was not the first to express this idea.

[†] https://www.ted.com/talks/tim_harford_how_frustration_can_make_us_more_creative/transcript?language=en.

Disruptions help us solve problems. They help us become more creative. But we don't feel that they're helping us. We feel that they are getting in the way, and so we resist.

—Tim Harford, economist and journalist

"Disruptions help us solve problems. They help us become more creative. But we don't feel that they're helping us. We feel that they are getting in the way, and so we resist." Harford tells a story of the musician and producer Brian Eno, who has worked with stars like David Bowie, Phil Collins, U2, and Coldplay on many of their albums. The way Eno brings out their creativity is to introduce "a mess" into their normal creative process, such as requiring members of the band to play different instruments. As Harford tells it, the groups hated Eno's messes. But album after album that Eno helped produce turned into massive successes, leading Harford to say, "Just because you don't like it doesn't mean it isn't helping you."

The greatest periods of growth are in these periods of dislocation and disconnection and reinvention.

—Bruce Feiler, author

Author Bruce Feiler is an authority on life transitions. In reflecting on the world we all face today, Feiler described it as a world where we all collectively experience what he calls "life-quakes."* Like Harford, Feiler is hugely optimistic about where the world is today and the opportunity a crisis can present. In his book *Life Is in the Transitions: Mastering Change at Any Age*, Feiler explains,

---

* https://www.linkedin.com/pulse/bruce-feiler-mastering-change-transitions-essential-parts-hempel/.

"Transitions are essential. They are the parts of life where we get better. We think of these periods as painful, uncomfortable, unpleasant periods we have to kind of grit or grind our way through. But in fact, the greatest periods of growth are in these periods of dislocation and disconnection and reinvention."[*] These are highly encouraging words we can all use to reframe the reality before us and to build our confidence.

We are only human, and when our world seems to turn on its head, we are often paralyzed with fear and anxiety. The best way to counter these feelings is to do what Harford suggests: step back, slow things down, and really focus on what is happening. Ask yourself:

- What can I do at this particular moment to prepare myself for the opportunities that will emerge once the pandemic clears?
- What actions can I take today and tomorrow that will increase my options for next week?
- Whom can I add to my board of directors to help my company?
- Whom can I add to my Personal Boardroom that can help me?
- Am I bringing a growth mindset to my learning and development so I know I can learn new skills?
- Are there opportunities in my volunteer work or in my hobbies for me to build new skills or see new career possibilities?

---

[*] https://www.brucefeiler.com/books-articles/life-is-in-the-transitions/.

If you need the inspiration to help you through challenging times, then I want you to remember Eva Rodriguez Labella and how she and her family responded to their life challenge. While nobody would have blamed them if they had become upset or frozen with fear and sorrow, how they responded is a model for all of us. The path they chose turned their world and their lives and careers into something even greater and more beautiful than they were before. More than they had imagined was possible.

How are you going to use this time of transition, change, and challenge in the world to come out better than you were before? How are you going to be better as a person, a professional, and an organization? Where in your hobbies, your life, and your activities might you find or create your "Strawberry Fairy?" What can you do as an employer so your employees can realize compelling careers? What can you learn and improve so when the next unexpected event arrives (and you know it's only a matter of time), you are better prepared?

Recall freeze, that improvisational game actors often play to fine-tune their creativity and ability to stay in the moment. Well, thanks to the coronavirus, the world has collectively frozen. Once it unfreezes, what new scene will you present to the audience?

Because the show must always go on.

A NOTE FROM THE AUTHOR

I fully expect this book will need to be updated soon, because the world of work is changing that fast. Therefore, I welcome your feedback, stories, and experiences, your successes and failures, and your lessons learned so we can work together and shape a better future of work.

Please join me in helping make the future of work less scary and intimidating and more human, rewarding, and energizing.

I look forward to hearing from you.

Steve Cadigan
December 2020
stevecadigan.com

ACKNOWLEDGMENTS

It is impossible to thank everyone who has helped me on my journey to complete this book. For years I would finish speaking at a conference or complete teaching a class and be approached by students and attendees asking me where they could find my book. I would always have to point to my brain and say, "It's in there." I am grateful to all of you for asking me the right question, for pushing me and encouraging me to share my ideas more broadly.

I want to thank the dozens of people whom I interviewed for this book and who shared their personal experiences and unique perspectives. I especially want to thank Eva Rodriguez Labella, who opened up her family and its fantastic journey with Yaiza, which continues today.

I want to thank my wife, Jenny, for being the guiding light of encouragement to make this happen and for allowing me the time and space to finish the book. I want to thank her for helping me get back on my feet when I needed to be lifted and especially for helping me rediscover my faith and holding my hand every day.

I also want to thank my friends Alan Webber and Adrian Simpson, who were the first people to grab me by the collar and tell me to get the book going.

I want to thank Laurie Dreyer, Zubin Chagpar, Linda and Dick Cadigan, and Christy Tonge for their tireless and thoughtful reviews and edits of my many drafts.

I would not have completed this book were it not for the constant support, drive, and encouragement of Beatriz Arana. She is a human hurricane of life and support as my PR and communication leader and CEO of Energia Communications. For years Beatriz encouraged and, when necessary, pushed me to undertake this mission, and I am so fortunate she believed in me and did not let go of her drive to make this happen.

I want to thank the incredibly talented ISDI Digital University global community for always filling my mind with new ideas, challenging me, and encouraging me to share them with the world. In particular, I want to thank my friends Amir Mashkoori, Nacho De Pinedo, Javier Zapatero, Rodrigo Miranda, and Arnaldo Munoz.

And last, I want to especially thank Thomas Lee, who was an extraordinary partner in this journey from start to finish. Tom helped me a great deal with his ideas, insights, research, and his way with words. The entire time Tom was with me on this project, he was also tackling some significant unexpected career changes of his own, *and* he was fighting a fierce battle with depression. Given the fact that this was my first time down the road of writing a book, I leaned on Tom a great deal for so many things. Even with his plate full, he was there for me every step of the way. Tom, I cannot thank you enough.

ABOUT THE AUTHOR

Steve Cadigan is a highly sought-after talent advisor to leaders and organizations across the globe. As Founder of his own Silicon Valley–based firm, Cadigan Talent Ventures, Steve advises a wide range of innovative organizations including Twitter, Eventbrite, Cisco, Intel, The Royal Bank of Scotland, Telefonica, Salesforce, and the BBC. He is also regularly retained by some of Silicon Valley's leading venture capital investment firms, such as Andreesen Horowitz, Index Ventures, Sequoia, and Greylock Partners, for his counsel on a wide range of talent topics. Steve speaks at conferences and teaches at major universities around the world. His work in helping shape the culture at LinkedIn led Stanford University to build a graduate-level class around this groundbreaking work. Steve is often asked to appear on global TV and is a frequent guest on Bloomberg West and CNBC. Throughout his career the teams, cultures, and organizations he has led and helped build have been recognized as exceptional, world-class performers by the *Wall Street Journal* and *Fortune* magazine.

Before launching his firm, Steve worked as an HR executive for over twenty-five years at a wide range of companies and industries, including ESPRIT, Fireman's Fund Insurance, Cisco Systems, PMC-Sierra, and Electronic Arts. His HR career was capped by serving as the first CHRO for LinkedIn from 2009 through 2012, taking the company from a private firm of four hundred employees to an IPO and helping set it up to be the powerhouse that it has become today.

Today, Steve serves on the boards of directors of three companies and also sits on the advisory boards of several other progressive organizations. His passion is helping leaders and companies build compelling talent strategies.

Over the course of his career, Steve has lived in Singapore, Canada, and the United States. He has interviewed, hired, coached, and mentored thousands of employees and leaders within a wide range of industries and geographies. This is what sets Steve apart from others who speak about the future of work. Steve has lived deep inside the world of work as an employee *and* as an employer. His experiences and achievements give him a unique and authoritative point of view, essential to all discussions about the future of work.

Steve lives in California with his family. He is the father of four boys and stepdad to two girls. When he is not speaking, teaching, or writing, you can find Steve coaching basketball, playing tennis, bodysurfing, driving his kids everywhere, or cheering them on at their activities.

Steve graduated from Wesleyan University with a bachelor's degree in history and received a master's degree in HR and organization development from the University of San Francisco.